Scoundrels & Eccentrics
of the Pacific

Scoundrels & Eccentrics
of the Pacific

John Dunmore

upstart press

A catalogue record for this book is available from the National Library of New Zealand.

ISBN 978-1-988516-21-9

An Upstart Press Book
Published in 2018 by Upstart Press Ltd
Level 4, 15 Huron Street, Takapuna 0622
Auckland, New Zealand

Designed by CVD Limited (www.cvdgraphics.nz)
Printed by Everbest Printing Co. Ltd., China

Contents

CARTE
de
L'OCÉANIE
ou
CINQUIÈME PARTIE DU MONDE

PAR

A. H. Brué, Géographe de S. A. R. Monsieur.

A PARIS

Chez L'AUTEUR, Rue des Maçons-Sorbonne No. 9,
et chez les principaux Marchands de Géographie.

Janvier 1820.

Longitude Orientale de Paris.

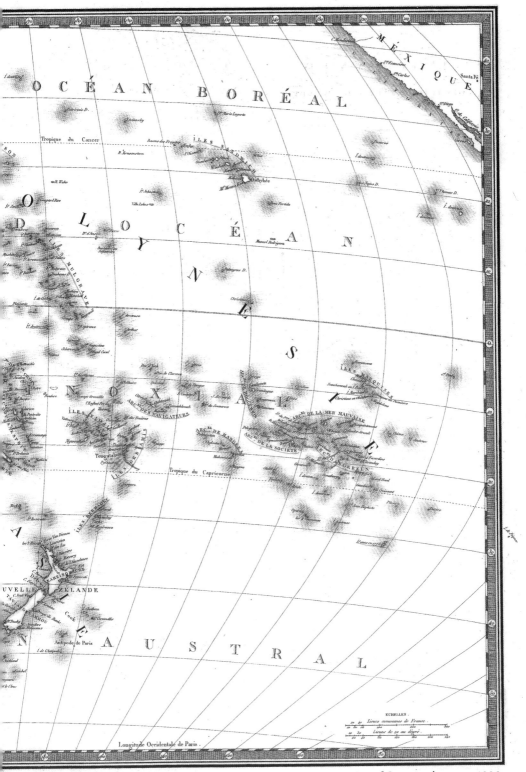

Map of Oceania drawn in 1820.

Foreword

The Pacific Ocean was the last region to be discovered and explored by Europeans. Even for those who lived along its shores, it was a world of mystery, danger and legend. Venturing into its vastness was often considered unwise, and in most cases the earliest settlers, mostly from Asia and its outlying islands, had sailed into it to avoid some invasion or some threat from their own region, hoping that they might find a new and safer home on an uninhabited island. This had taken centuries and the islands of the Pacific eventually each presented their own private world, with their own legends, their way of life and their traditions.

The Europeans came much later, with discoveries, often unexpected, gradual exploration, followed by venturesome trade, settlement, exploitation and colonisation. The great powers tried to exclude each other and create their own empire – first the Spanish and the Dutch, then the British, the French, the Germans and in time the Japanese. But in between, there were raiders, pirates, thieves, private individuals who worked and often cheated in the hope of building their own little world, exploiting an ocean which was only slowly being controlled and brought into the theoretical orderliness that dominated the rest of the world.

This is a small collection of the tales that have been told of the men, and in some cases the women, who sought to benefit from the discoveries of the early explorers, scoundrels and rogues with little conscience but great craftiness, and of those who as a result found themselves victims of situations they could hardly imagine. It shows that humankind, in whatever period and whatever part of the world, may have its heroes, but it always has its villains.

1

Chinese Explorer or Conman?

To the people who lived along the coasts, the Pacific Ocean was the edge of the world. They stared out at this immensity of water, sometimes placid, more often angry, as they might at eternity itself. It might hold promise for a few; for some it was a world of legend, with mythical heroes and monsters, but it held terror for most. Wise indeed were those who merely took it for granted, something about which one did not speculate, a foreign world that was incomprehensible or meaningless. One could fish and sail along the shore, usually in some frail craft, but one would be unwise to venture out too far, out of sight of land, for one might never return.

To the Chinese, living in what most believed was the centre of the world, the Middle Kingdom, the sea was one of the limits of the universe. No one could live out there, certainly not human beings. It was a world of strange aliens, possibly the abode of the Immortals, but certainly one of mystery. For centuries, the Chinese built their empire across Asia, leaving the ocean to itself.

Those who lived close to the great rivers, such as the Yangtze and the Yellow River, the Huang He, and saw them roaring towards the ocean, swollen by heavy inland rains, overflowing and flooding into the rice fields, believed that there was a giant maelstrom out in the ocean, the Wei Lu, a great hole into which poured the water, taking with it any unfortunate craft that had ventured too close to it. If there was no such plughole, then the waters would rise up everywhere and flood the world. It was much more logical to believe in this Wei Lu, where the waters poured down into the earth and, after being cleansed in the underworld, re-emerged as bubbling springs in the mountain ranges or rose in spiralling clouds over the horizon. This belief remained widely held for centuries, because as late as the 13th century of the modern era the historian Chau Ju Kua, the author of *Zhu Fan Zhi*, or "*A Description of Barbarous People*", reminded his readers of the Great Hole of Wei Lu, where waters drain "into the world from which men do not return".

The old legends also spoke of Fu Sang, a paradise somewhere beyond the horizon, a magical place where enchanters dwelt, where silkworms grew two metres long, and where the herb of eternal youth might be found. Immortality is a theme that was often found in the old legends that were narrated around the fire or discussed in temples.

Stories these might be, but some began to dream of going to see for themselves. Around the year 219 B.C., the Emperor Shi Huang Ti raised the question with one of his courtiers, Hsu Fu, or Xu Fu, who had a reputation as a skilled man and also as a sorcerer. Shi Huang Ti could look back on his own life with a great deal of satisfaction: he had started in 245 B.C. as a mere local ruler, but in less than 20 years he had unified China under his rule. He had reorganised the country, extended its frontier to the edges of Vietnam and Korea, had had a great wall built to keep out intruders, and was now ruling a vast empire with great efficiency

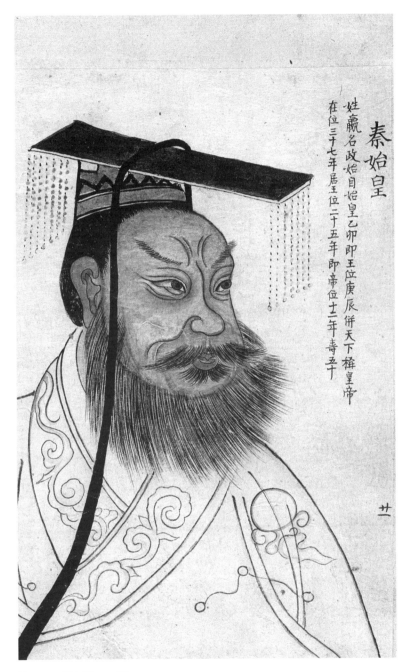

秦始皇

在位三十七年居王位二十五年即帝位十二年壽五十

姓嬴名政始目始皇乙卯即王位庚辰併天下稱皇帝

廿

Emperor Shi Huang Ti

and ruthlessness. His dynasty, the Qin or Ch'in, would give the country its name, and as a ruler he was both admired and feared.

However, one thing worried him, as he grew older, and that was the prospect of death. His name, he knew, would become immortal, his body would be preserved in a great mausoleum and guarded by an army of small soldier-like figurines, but his life would have ended, and he would know nothing of what the future might hold. He had heard, however, like most of the Chinese, of wondrous islands far off in the Pacific Ocean, where there grew a magic herb that ensured eternal life. The plant of immortality might be a myth, but it was worth a try, a feeling that grew after at least one assassination attempt and the onset of middle age. His courtier suggested that he could sail off in the name of the emperor, using his own great talents to deal with whatever magic islands he might encounter. Shi Huang Ti agreed and supplied him with the ships, made mostly of bamboo, and the crews and supplies he would need.

Hsu Fu is reported to have set out on his first expedition early in the year 219 B.C. He is said to have sailed from the ancient city of Lang Yu in Shantung province with a small fleet of large bamboo ships and to have begun his search for the islands where the Immortals lived, with the mission of persuading them to share their wonderful herb to preserve the life of the great Chinese emperor. He probably thought it a wise move, as he was only in his early thirties and he feared the struggles for succession that would inevitably occur after the emperor's death and which, as one of the elderly ruler's prized courtiers, would probably cost him his life.

There was no sign of him for almost a year, and most of the courtiers who knew about the enterprise assumed that he had been caught by the currents and driven into Wei Lu, or else fallen victim to some other monsters who were believed to inhabit islands of the

Pacific. But he did reappear one day and reported that, after many a struggle, he had discovered an island he said was called Peng Lai and a palace known as the Chich Cheng, guarded by a fearsome dragon, and housing a powerful ruler whom he was finally allowed to meet. He presented the gifts he had brought and paid homage to the powerful Immortal on behalf of the emperor. But he had not succeeded in obtaining any of the sacred plants. The ruling magician knew how valuable the herb was, but he wanted more than Hsu Fu had brought – and he stressed that it needed to be well guarded on the voyage back to China, so that no unworthy person, no one in fact other than the emperor, could receive that marvellous plant. He had heard of the great Ch'in empire and its achievements, and he asked for Chinese young men of noble lineage, together with maidens of similar status and a number of skilled artisans. They would serve his own kingdom, learn his own magical skills and ensure the safety of the invaluable herb of immortality.

It seemed a straightforward proposition, and the emperor was soon persuaded. He gave Hsu Fu 3,000 young men and women – some say the number was even greater – and all the artisans and guards he needed. He added an ample supply of food and samples of Chinese artefacts, as well as personal gifts for the ruler, now referred to as the Great Magician of the Sea. Re-equipped and supplied with new rafts, Hsu Fu sailed away. He was never seen again, at least not by the emperor who died within a year or so of his departure. There was no magic herb for him, and the Qin dynasty collapsed a few years later in widespread disorder and endless plots and counterplots. It sounds to us as though Hsu Fu had found an attractive island somewhere, and that he planned to found a colony there. There might well be no magic herb at all, but Emperor Shih Huang Ti, a realist to the end, might have believed that if that was the case Hsu Fu in his colony would become his vassal, and if there was no herb of longevity, there would be at least an annual tribute. He was disappointed. His gamble did not pay.

According to most tales, Hsu Fu was never heard of again. But there are versions stating that Hsu Fu did return a few months later, saying that all was well and that the Great Magician of the Sea was keeping his promise to supply the plants, but that they were too precious to be taken to China without more armed guards powerful and numerous enough to protect them from any strangers or any of the island rulers that lay on the road back. By now, however, Shi Huang Ti was dead, and his heirs were not interested. Hsu Fu disappeared, supposedly returning to Peng Lai to persuade the Great Magician to relent.

Hsu Fu was undoubtedly a skilled navigator and there has been a fair amount of speculation over the years about the actual route he followed. In 1993, the Englishman Tim Severin attempted to prove that a bamboo raft could actually cross the Pacific. He sailed from Vietnam and covered several thousand miles before his vessel – which he had named the *Hsu Fu* – finally disintegrated. It is unlikely that the real Hsu Fu ever sailed to America – a continent the ancient Chinese knew nothing about – but it is fairly certain that he sailed to several large Pacific islands and was setting up his own kingdom on one of them.

Chinese mythology does mention a number of islands that lay out in the ocean – away from the dangerous Wei Lu – such as the kingdom of Queen Pimiko, in a country called Wa. It is mentioned in an ancient Chinese chronicle, the *Hou Han Shu*, compiled around the fifth century, and was probably situated in southern Japan. "Pimiko" is possibly a corrupted version of *himeko*, an archaic Japanese word meaning "princess". When a princess, she remained unmarried, busying herself instead with magic and sorcery, and bewitching the populace, whereupon she became their queen. She kept 1,000 female attendants at her court, but few of the people ever saw her. There was only one man there, who was in charge of her wardrobe and her meals, and who acted as her means of communication. She lived in a palace surrounded by towers and stockades, defended by armed guards.

A thousand miles to the south of this queen's land, there was another land, where dwarfs lived. Its inhabitants were no more than three or four feet high. Then to the south-east, much further off – as the journey, some said, took a year – one came to the land of the Naked People, and then to the country of the Black-Teethed Men. These stories may sound like imaginary myths, but they suggest some knowledge of the islands of Micronesia and Melanesia, where clothing can be regarded as skimpy indeed, and of some of the Philippines, where betelnut chewing is common and turns the teeth a distinctive and, to outsiders, startling black.

But it is now generally accepted that Hsu Fu travelled to what is now Japan. It is relatively close to the Chinese mainland, particularly to Shantung province, from which he had set out, and Hsu Fu is in fact recognised as one of the founders of early Japan. His arrival coincided with changes in agricultural techniques, and his name is included in several documents about early Japan. He is sometimes called "the God of Farming", "the God of Medicine" and "the God of Silk". Memorials to him can be found in several places, including a Ku Shu Research Institute attached to a local teachers' college. His influence on early Japanese culture and trade is the subject of current research, including his possible influence on the Shinto religion. In a totally different context, he was used as a character in the *Marvel Comics* in 2011. . .

Hsu Fu was undeniably a skilled navigator, driving a small fleet of ships and rafts made largely of bamboo. As Tim Severin showed, they would not have survived a lengthy journey, and it is likely that some of them disintegrated before Hsu Fu reached his goal. But he is also a perfect model for the modern scammer. His modern equivalent uses mail, or more usually email. Recipients, no doubt numerous and spread across the world, receive a plea from someone who needs help to get a large family fortune out of the country to prevent the current rulers from getting their hands on it. And if the scammer succeeds in getting help from a gullible victim, he will return to try to get more.

Hsu Fu may have failed in his third endeavour, not because the Chinese emperor had lost faith in him, but because the elderly ruler had died. The herb of immortality had come too late for him. Early Japan may well have benefited from the enterprise, as had Hsu Fu, entering history as a man who was as skilled as he was unscrupulous. Either way, the Chinese cannot fail to admire him, his work and to some extent his long-term achievements.

2

Pirates and Their Ilk

*P*iracy has existed from the earliest times, whether the victims were fishermen who had ventured too far from the shore, or small merchantmen taking their wares to the nearest port. Like highwaymen hiding in forests, ready to pounce on any prey they could find, the pirates roamed through the open seas, looking for a passing ship they could attack. Hence the term "corsair", from the French *course* (a run), which came into use in the Middle Ages, and gives the impression of a fast animal chasing its weaker prey. "Pirates" was a broader term that dated back to early Greece and usually referred to a sea robber in and around the Mediterranean Sea. William Shakespeare often refers to pirates, whom he calls "salt-water thieves". The term has lasted through time and today refers to anyone stealing someone's property, including writings, music or drama, not roaming the sea, as of old, but the airwaves.

"Buccaneers" were usually pirates who were based in and around the Caribbean Sea, and the term is derived from their basic food supplies of hard dried meat, *boucan* in French. "Privateers" applied, in some respect, to a higher grade of pirates, who had received, formally or informally, permission to attack and capture roaming ships, including merchantmen, belonging to an enemy nation. They were, in effect, acting as a private branch of the navy, fighting the enemy, but in fact, robbing passing ships rather than attacking units of a foreign fleet. However, with the major European powers, Britain, France, Spain, the Netherlands, being so often at war, the line of demarcation between a pirate and a privateer is often blurred.

The pirates found the relatively unknown Pacific Ocean a valuable field of action, and the rivalry between Spain – which in the early years had attempted to claim it as "the Spanish Lake" – and the other powers provided a valuable background to their activities. Exploration could be put forward as an excuse for their incursions, and the antagonism of the Spaniards provided the excuse for violence and robbery. Thus, although the English might disagree, the Spanish viewed Francis Drake as a mere pirate, to be hanged if caught. He had the covert protection of Queen Elizabeth I, and had raided Spanish settlements in the West Indies in the

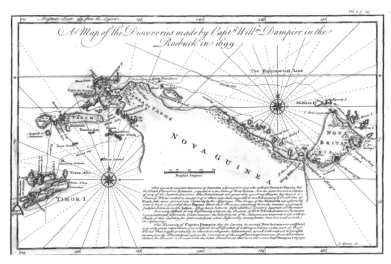

Although William Dampier can be regarded as a pirate, his contribution to European knowledge of the Pacific world and to cartography is considerable, as his map of 1699 shows.

early 1570s. However, he really wanted to sail into the Pacific and succeeded in doing so by passing through the Straits of Magellan at the southern tip of South America with his ship the *Pelican* (later renamed the *Golden Hind*) in October 1578. He began raiding Spanish settlements along the coast of Chile and Peru, venturing as far as northern California, collecting a rich booty and destroying ships and small settlements. He had hoped to discover a north-west passage back into the Atlantic, the equivalent of the Straits of Magellan, but failed and returned to England by way of the Cape of Good Hope, becoming the first English captain to complete a voyage around the world. He was back in Britain by September 1580, and the Queen, overcoming her fear that this might upset the Spanish government, went on board his ship and knighted him.

However, the richest prize in Pacific waters at that time was the Spanish galleon, a large ship heavily laden with gold and other precious materials, which the Spanish traditionally sent annually from the Philippines to Mexico, and which returned to Manila after being refitted and restocked in Acapulco. Another famous English captain – or privateer – Thomas Cavendish, succeeded in capturing one, the *Santa Ana*, off the coast of California in 1587. His return to England with the riches he had looted attracted a great deal of attention, and encouraged others to follow suit. Richard Hawkins was one such. He was a youngish man of some status, being the son of an admiral, and he had once served under Drake and captained a ship in the fight against the Spanish Armada. He sailed into the Pacific in 1594 in command of a privateer vessel, the quaintly named *Dainty*, merely intending, he later claimed, to carry out a voyage of exploration. However, his main achievement was the sacking and plundering of the major port of Valparaiso, after which he continued on his way north, looking for more loot, but he was defeated and captured by two Spanish ships. He was taken in chains to Spain and not released until 1602. However, shortly after his return he was knighted and elected to Parliament. Ironically, he was then appointed vice-admiral for Devon, a post which involved keeping the English Channel free of roving pirates. A few years later, he sailed to the Mediterranean to help clear the trading routes of Algerian corsairs.

The Caribbean was a region where piracy thrived, but it also opened the way to the Pacific – or the Great South Sea, as it was also known – by way of the Isthmus of Panama. William Dampier, who had crossed the isthmus in 1679 with a group of buccaneers and plundered the Spanish settlements around the coast, alternated between buccaneering in the Caribbean and engaging in a mixture of piracy and exploration on the Pacific side. He gained considerable fame through this, and was later sent on an official voyage of exploration around Australia and New Guinea, the first Englishman known to have set foot on Australian soil.

Before Dampier, however, a much less reputable buccaneer, Henry Morgan, had crossed the isthmus and begun raiding the Spanish Pacific settlements. A Welshman of good standing, he was related to high-ranking military officers, including an uncle who had led the English raid on Jamaica in 1655. He carried out a number of raids on Spanish possessions in the Caribbean and on the coast of Venezuela, bringing back a great haul of gold and silver, some being the product of ransoms obtained from Spanish garrisons, the rest simply stolen from ports or passing ships. Then, in 1670, he assembled a small fleet to attack Panama, stole whatever could be found and set the town on fire. As it turned out, England and Spain were at peace at the time, and the Spanish made a formal protest to the English authorities. Henry Morgan and the then governor of Jamaica were recalled to London, but were easily forgiven. A frequent excuse was that, given the lack of communication once a ship had left its home port, the sailors were unable to discover that hostilities between the various countries had ceased. Morgan was eventually sent back to Jamaica with a knighthood and the post of Lieutenant-Governor. He died in 1688.

The rivalry between England and Spain had not taken long to revive, and other buccaneers made their way across the Isthmus of Panama, hoping to raid Spanish outposts. Bartholomew Sharp was a 30-year-old buccaneer admired

William Dampier

by his followers both for his skill and his ruthlessness. In 1680, he sailed with captains, such as John Coxon, Basil Ringrose and Richard Sawkins, taking over command of the small fleet when Sawkins was killed. Although he is often regarded as a leading figure among buccaneers of the time, his leadership was merely due to circumstances, his temporary popularity among the other raiders and, in his case, his total disregard for the Spanish settlers and sailors he encountered. The present-day cathedral of La Serena in Chile bears a plaque stating that it was built to replace the original church destroyed when Bartholomew Sharp and his men ransacked the township. They then captured a Spanish ship of some 400 tons, named *La Santissima Trinidad* (The Most Holy

Trinity), which they renamed the *Trinity*, and carried on attacking settlements and Spanish vessels, burning and stealing as they went. Sharp continued as leader until the *Trinity* put into one of the Juan Fernandez Islands, where a mutiny occurred and he was replaced by another buccaneer, John Watling. The new leader planned an attack on the town of Arica in northern Chile that was believed to contain great treasures. However, the authorities in Lima, pre-warned, had despatched a strong force to defend it. Watling was among those killed in the ensuing battle, and Bartholomew Sharp was once again elected leader. In spite of further disputes and mutinies, he remained in charge, and took the *Trinity* south and around Cape Horn into the Atlantic, having carried out a number of raids on coastal ports and villages, usually burning them down, and capturing and destroying an estimated 25 Spanish vessels.

Sharp and some of his followers eventually made their way to London, bringing some valuable charts of the Pacific area which they had stolen from their Spanish victims. The English geographers were impressed, but Sharp found them even more valuable when he was arrested in May 1682, following a formal complaint of peacetime piracy laid against him and several others by the Spanish ambassador. The High Court of the Admiralty acquitted him, probably under some pressure from King Charles II who had seen and admired the charts, and who eventually granted Sharp a commission in the Royal Navy. This did not greatly interest Sharp, who returned to the Caribbean and resumed his activities as a buccaneer. However, the golden age of piracy was coming to an end in the region, and he fled to some Danish-controlled islands, escaping his debtors. He was eventually imprisoned there and died in 1702.

His fame and that of other pirates of his day is owed in great part to a best-selling work published in London in 1684 by Basil

Ringrose, *Bucaniers of America: The Second Volume Containing The Dangerous Voyage and Bold Attempts of Captain Bartholomew Sharp and Others . . .* Other works were written about the buccaneers of the Caribbean and the west coast of America, frequently embroidered with tales of sea monsters and local inhabitants, so that the brutality and cruelty which marked the lives of the pirates is often toned down, and the term "pirates of the South Seas" acquired in time a certain charm and popularity.

William Dampier was one of those who benefited from the broad image of a South Sea filled with adventures and acts of heroism. Dampier had sailed for years in the Atlantic and across the Pacific Ocean, going to the Philippines and China, then south towards Australia. On his return to England, he wrote an account of his adventures in a highly successful work, *A New Voyage Round the World*, published in 1697. He had been guided by geographers and hydrographers, so that his account was not too romanticised and could be dedicated to the Earl of Halifax who was president of the Royal Society. Four new editions quickly followed, with translations into French, Dutch and German. A new version, *Voyages and Descriptions*, appeared in 1699, and an account of his later travels, *A Voyage to New Holland*, in 1703. Although essentially a pirate, Dampier was also recognised as a skilled navigator. His talents as a commander were far more limited. He was renowned for his ill-temper and his brutality towards his colleagues and his crews, not to mention Spanish sailors and settlers. However, he was appointed by the Admiralty to lead an expedition of exploration in the New Guinea and Australian areas. He sailed in HMS *Roebuck* and carried out some creditable work of exploration, but conditions on board were bad and the ship was in a poor condition. The worm-ridden *Roebuck* sank off Ascension Island on the journey home. Dampier and most of the crew eventually made their way back to England, but Dampier had to face two court-martials: one for the loss of the vessel, the other for his behaviour as captain. He was banned from further commands in the navy, and returned to buccaneering, for which he was far more suited.

In September 1703, he joined a privateering expedition, commanding the *St George*, and sailed once more towards the Spanish settlements in the Pacific, together with another privateer, the *Cinque Ports*. The expedition was again plagued by mutinies and desertions, and the *Cinque Ports'* master, Alexander Selkirk, who could not stand the endless quarrels, asked to be set ashore on Juan Fernandez Island, where he remained alone until rescued in 1709, eventually becoming famous as the model for Robinson Crusoe, a creation of Daniel Defoe, the initiator of wildly popular similar stories about castaways and desert islands. Back in England, William Dampier had had to cope with the usual complaints and threats of legal proceedings, but he managed to be appointed pilot to an expedition being planned by certain Bristol merchants who hoped to capture the great "Manila galleons" that sailed between Acapulco and Manila. Its commander was to be a Bristol sailor named Woodes Rogers, and the situation seemed favourable for the undertaking, as relations between Spain and England had once again turned bad, resulting in French raids against merchantmen, including some from Bristol who had links with Woodes Rogers.

Two vessels, the *Duke* and the *Duchess*, were bought for the expedition, and official documents were obtained allowing Rogers to carry out a privateering expedition against the French "or others of Her Majesty's enemies", as against mere acts of piracy against any ships they met. The expedition set sail on 2 August 1708, making first for Cork in Ireland, where it loaded fresh supplies and replaced

Depiction of William Dampier in a small open boat near Aceh (Indonesia), 1698.

about 40 sailors who had already mutinied and deserted. An early problem was Woodes Rogers' refusal to attack a passing ship, which would have provided some welcome treasure for his crewmen, but as it was a Swedish vessel it would have meant an act of straightforward piracy, as against the permissible privateering. They were luckier as they approached Tenerife in the Canary Islands and captured a small Spanish barque, which they were able to ransom for gold and much-needed food and wine. They then went south to round Cape Horn and make their way into the Pacific, aiming first at the Juan Fernandez Islands. It was a hard struggle and a number of men died of scurvy or accidents. They were relieved, therefore, when on 31 January 1709, a fire appeared on the island. It turned out to be a bonfire lit by Alexander Selkirk who was still waiting to be rescued.

They spent a fortnight on the island, greatly assisted by Selkirk who showed them where food and water could be obtained, and who cooked meals for the sick men aboard. He was happy to be taken as second mate on the *Duke*, and the expedition went on its way towards the island of Lobos and the port of Guayaquil on the coast of Ecuador, capturing three Spanish merchant ships on the way. Guayaquil was a prosperous port and trading centre, which had been raided by Dutch, English and French pirates on several occasions. The town was consequently well organised to fight off further raids, but Rogers and his men succeeded in burning down a number of houses and capturing a fair amount of loot. The invaders, however, were really after a ransom, offering to spare the town if adequate payment was made. Negotiations took over a fortnight, but Rogers and his men finally agreed on what the Spaniards were willing to pay, and they sailed on to the Galapagos Islands to repair their ships and prepare for their battle against a Manila galleon. This involved sailing along the coast of Mexico and on to Cape San Lucas in California. The wait was a long one: it was not until late December that a vessel appeared that turned out to be their longed-for prey, the *Nuestra Senora de la Encarnacion y Desengano*. But the galleon turned out to be too strong for Woodes Rogers' raiders, and after a lengthy struggle, the attempt to capture it and the riches it carried was abandoned, although some ransom was agreed on to end the fighting.

It had been a costly series of operations and Woodes Rogers, who had himself been wounded in one of the sea fights and who had actually lost his brother in a battle, decided to sail away from the Americas and make his way to Batavia by way of Guam. The Dutch accepted their presence after some hesitation, as their visit was infringing the monopoly that the Dutch had been careful to preserve, and Rogers' ships were repaired, stocks of food were loaded and 17 men were recruited to make up in part for the losses sustained as a result of battles or sickness. They left on 24 October, making their way home by way of the Cape of Good Hope and, having sailed in the company of several Dutch vessels, they reached Holland at the end of July 1711. Although the Dutch East Indies Company proved hostile and started legal proceedings against Rogers, he was allowed to go on to England and finally anchored in the Thames on 14 October 1711.

The Dutch received some payment in settlement of their claim, the crew were paid off, although most of them felt the amount they received was inadequate for their work and suffering, while Rogers found that the profits from his voyage were hardly sufficient to pay off the debts his family had incurred in his absence. However, as mentioned, he published a highly successful account of his journey. After a failed attempt to colonise the island of Madagascar he was appointed Governor of the Bahamas. Since this was in the Caribbean, a hotbed of pirates, he had to deal with the chaotic situation the sea robbers had created and which continued to worsen as time went by. His position was semi-official, as he was also working on behalf of traders affected by the ongoing piracy. He struggled for several years, endeavouring to cope with his opponents and running up debts. He returned to England, was imprisoned for a while for debts, was pardoned and returned to the West Indies, where he died, exhausted and helpless, in July 1732. William Dampier who had been his skilled assistant on his voyage to the Pacific had predeceased him, dying similarly worn out and destitute in 1715.

As the 18th century progressed, the Pacific Ocean became better known, more frequented and safe from the worst excesses of pirates. Improved relations with Spain meant that privateers were no longer trying to work their way around Cape Horn and along the South American coast. Raids on places such as Chile, Peru and Panama had become more difficult as the Spanish settlements increased in size and built stronger defences. The chaotic world of the early Caribbean was now better policed as traders and colonists put increased pressure on their home countries to restructure their administrative systems, which had been ineffective for so long, due not only to incompetence and inadequate resources, but also to bribery.

Voyages of exploration brought the Pacific into the public eye. The Spanish and the Dutch had dominated in the 16th and 17th centuries, but Britain and France led the way during the 18th. Following the travels and narratives of men like Dampier and Rogers, major undertakings were promoted by scientific societies and trading companies, resulting in the voyages of John Byron in 1764, Samuel Wallis and Philip Carteret in 1766–68, James Cook in 1768, 1772 and 1776, and the French expeditions of Louis-Antoine de Bougainville in 1766, Jean-Francois de Surville in 1769, Jean-Francois de la Perouse in 1786 and Jules Dumont d'Urville in 1822, 1825 and 1837. The Spanish and the Russians also sent out scientific and other expeditions in the late 18th and early 19th centuries. The result was a vastly increased interest not only by scientists and geographers, but also by politicians, which led to the elimination of the belief in the existence of a vast southern continent, and in the improvement and rounding off of charts and world maps. Trade developed between the various islands, and a British colony was founded in Australia in 1788, the so-called First Fleet of 11 ships bringing convicts, soldiers and settlers to New South Wales. It could be argued that the fleet, which returned after spending some time exploring and trading in the Pacific, had pioneered the China trade and the fur trade. Missionaries soon followed, both Protestants and Catholics, settling on various islands.

*   *   *

By the middle of the 19th century, the Pacific Ocean could be said to be part of the broader world, with British, French, Dutch and German colonies. The pirates who had infested the main trade lines in earlier years disappeared: they had lost their bases in the Caribbean, the western coast of the Americas was too well defended, and there were now too many ships, trading, exploring, carrying European settlers and protecting European-controlled bases, for the sea robbers to venture into what had once been a vast open and practically unknown ocean. But there were a few cases in modern times when sea captains whom one can describe as pirates sailed in search of prey – the occasion that offered itself, although briefly, was war in Europe.

Germany had established a few colonies in the Pacific Ocean, ill-defended in case of a major conflict, and when the First World War broke out, New Zealand despatched a force to take over German Samoa, while Australia occupied the German settlements in New Guinea and the Bismarck Archipelago. Japan had joined the Allies and captured a German outpost on the China Coast and a number of islands in the Marianas, the Palaus and the Carolines. A German naval squadron under the command of Admiral Maximilian Von Spee attacked the French colony of Tahiti and the British-held island of Fanning and defeated a British squadron off the coast of Chile, but it was on its way to the Atlantic and in December it was itself destroyed in a battle off the Falkland Islands. Thus, by the end of 1914, the Pacific Ocean was free of German forces. However, the occasional raider making its way into the Pacific could be termed a privateer, having both a commission from the relevant government and a clear intent to attack a passing trader or an unprotected coastal settlement.

The most famous of these is Felix Von Luckner, the captain of the *Seeadler* (Sea Eagle), a three-masted sailing ship with guns, machine guns and auxiliary engines carefully hidden from view. Flying a Norwegian flag, it had escaped the British blockade and sailed into the Atlantic. In early 1917, it had sunk its first prey, a collier on its way from Cardiff to Buenos Aires, and the following day captured a steamer returning from Madagascar. Another ten vessels, French, Canadian, Italian and British, were captured and sunk during the next three months. Von Luckner, however, was not a privateer of the old school – who would have thrown his prisoners overboard or cut their throats – but a relatively kind man who kept his prisoners safe on board. This resulted in overcrowding and when he captured a French four-masted barque, the *Cambronne*, he transferred the prisoners to her and allowed her to sail away, having earlier reduced its sails to ensure it could only move away slowly, giving time for the *Seeadler* to vanish.

By now, the Royal Navy was actively searching for the privateer, who became known in time as the *Seeteufel* (Sea Devil), and his crew as the *Piraten des Kaisers* (The Kaiser's Pirates).

SMS Seeadler, *Von Luckner's vessel, in the South Seas.*

Von Luckner therefore sailed away into the Pacific Ocean, heading along the coast of Chile and sinking several vessels, including some flying the American flag, as the United States had now entered the war on the side of the Allies. However, the *Seeadler* by now needed repairs, but could not risk putting into a Chilean or Peruvian port. Von Luckner therefore sailed into the open sea, reaching the Society Islands and finding a refuge in a small, practically uninhabited atoll, Maupihaa. Unfortunately, a heavy storm or, as some have suggested, a tsunami, struck the atoll and the *Seeadler* was wrecked on the reef. Von Luckner constructed a longboat and started on his way to Fiji where he hoped to capture another vessel. But this was a journey of some 2,500 kilometres, and the voyage was a strain on his men. In time they reached the island of Atiu in the Cook Islands and then went on to Aitutaki with its large lagoon. They were able to obtain some food, mostly coconuts, although their arrival caused some suspicion among the few residents who found it hard to believe that they were Dutch and Norwegian sailors. They nevertheless proceeded towards Fiji, always hoping that they might encounter a small vessel they could capture and take back to Maupihaa. They reached Wakaya Island, part of the Fiji group, but their journey had come to an end: they were arrested, taken to the capital of Fiji, and Von Luckner was sent to a small prison camp on the island of Motuihe in the Hauraki Gulf in New Zealand.

It might be expected that Von Luckner and the few Germans who had arrived with him would be satisfied to await the end of the war, which was now in its fourth year, and indeed that is the image he presented to the camp's commander, Lieutenant-Colonel Turner. The prisoners were allowed to walk about the island, keep chickens and even prepare a Christmas concert. But Von Luckner had other ideas, and in December 1917 he and ten others stole the commander's motor launch, having first cut the island's telephone wires, thus isolating it and giving them time to escape.

They got as far as the Mercury Islands, off the north-eastern coast, hoping to capture a vessel suitable for sailing to South America. Von Luckner succeeded in seizing a coastal trader, the *Moa*, taking prisoner its captain and five crewmen. He reached the

Kermadec Islands, some 900 kilometres away, claiming one of the islands for Germany and raising a German flag he had smuggled with him. At this point, however, his good fortune ran out, and a New Zealand armed vessel, the *Iris*, sent after him, finally captured him and his men, and returned them to prison in New Zealand.

Like other piratical sailors before him, Von Luckner wrote an account of his adventures, published in German in 1926, which proved a bestseller, although unlike the writings of Dampier and Rogers they did not contribute much to the knowledge of the Pacific. They did, however, help to create an image that has lasted, given rise to a German television series, and led to the eventual foundation of the Von Luckner Society. He died in Sweden in 1966, aged 84.

The Second World War also gave rise to minor attempts at piracy. However, the framework was totally changed by the role of Japan, which this time was on the opposing side and dominated the war in the Pacific Ocean. In addition, the aeroplane had become a major factor in the war and scientific developments, such as radio-location and wireless transmission, had changed the risks for ships in Pacific waters. Nevertheless, there were cases of disguised vessels and daring raiders who recall the corsairs of earlier times.

Disguising a warship as a merchantman can be said to be breaking the rules of war. However strange it might sound to have a set of rule for waging war, there had been for many years the understanding that those who were engaged in waging war should wear a uniform to distinguish them from civilians. The term *franc-tireur* (free shooter) was used to describe men who fought against the enemy invader without belonging to any regiment or military group. If captured, they were often shot as simple criminals. The Franco-Prussian war of 1870–71 had brought the term into prominence, as most free shooters were associated with rifle clubs whose members carried out a number of attacks on the German troops, including blowing up the Moselle railway bridge at Fontenoy in January 1871 and holding up the German advance at Chateaudun. The First World War saw less of these activities, as the lines between the combatants were more precisely outlined by the trenches and universal conscription ensured that all men of appropriate age were called up for military service.

It may be surprising therefore to find that, long before the outbreak of the Second World War, the Germans had been preparing plans for what they called auxiliary cruisers – warships that would be disguised as merchantmen and wage war on trading vessels, having concealed guns and a crew of well-trained naval personnel. When Hitler came to power in 1933, he set aside the disarmament agreements that followed the First World War, left the League of Nations, and proceeded to reorganise and rearm the German state. This led to the development of a plan devised by naval officers to develop ships that looked like merchantmen, but could swiftly be transformed into wartime raiders. A dozen such ships were built, the aim being largely to carry out raids in the Atlantic, to disrupt the supplies being sent to Britain and France. Several of these raiders, however, moved into the Pacific.

The raider *Orion* was one of the first to operate around Australia and New Zealand, laying mines off the Hauraki Gulf in the hope of sinking ships bound to or from Auckland. The result was the sinking of the liner *Niagara* on 19 June 1940 and of the minesweeper *Puriri* in May 1941. The time difference between the two tragedies illustrates the dangerous effect of mines, which could float on for months, long after the departure of the ship that had unloaded them. The loss of the *Niagara* had made it clear that there was a raider operating in the Pacific, and a search began. However, the *Orion* had by then sailed towards the Coral Sea and the islands of Polynesia, and succeeded in capturing and destroying several merchantmen. British sailors who survived the sinkings were kept on board as prisoners, but some were transferred to other disguised German raiders which by now had entered the Pacific. They became known as the Far East Squadron, and included a large cargo ship, the *Kulmerland*, acting as a supply vessel, and others helping to refuel the raiders. To make it more difficult for the Allies to catch the raiders, the Germans at times repainted their ships and altered the appearance of their decks.

The capture of isolated cargo ships was a welcome event for the Germans who could take over and often share among themselves the cargo they carried. One such case was the capture in November 1940 of the small New Zealand steamer, the *Holmwood*, which was taking a supply of sheep and wool from Waitangi to Lyttelton – the sheep were brought over to the raiders before the ship was sunk. But not long after this event, the *Orion* and the *Komet* sank the large liner *Rangitane*, on her way from Auckland to Liverpool via the Panama Canal, carrying cargo but, more importantly, over a hundred passengers, some leaving for military service in Europe, but the majority mere civilians, including women. A number of those were wounded in the brief shelling, making their transfer over to the raiders a difficult task. The *Rangitane* was then scuttled by the Germans.

The four main German warships that carried out raids in the Pacific and Indian oceans were eventually sunk. The *Kormoran*, disguised at the time as a Dutch trader called the *Straat Malakka*, destroyed the Australian cruiser *Sydney* in November 1941, but had caught fire in the fight and was scuttled off the coast of Western

Australia. The *Pinguin* was sunk in the Indian Ocean in May 1941. The *Komet*, after carrying out a series of raids in the Pacific, returned to Germany and, in October 1942, having been refitted, set out on a second voyage, disguised as a merchantman named the *Sperrbrecker*, but was caught and sunk in the English Channel. The *Orion* also managed to make her way back to Germany, but was eventually destroyed in the Baltic Sea towards the end of the war. In all, these four ships had sunk 50 ships. After 1942, with the Allies increasingly aware of their plans and with the entry of Japan and the United States into the conflict, German raids in the Pacific Ocean became impractical and the German navy put an end to any further plans for action in that distant part of the world.

Piracy in earlier times had included, as an important element, the stealing of gold and other valuables, to be kept by the pirates themselves in most cases, but also to be handed to the state in the case of privateers. During the Second World War, however, the presence of German raiders disguising themselves as harmless merchant ships or flying the colours of different countries resembles the work of partisans and *francs-tireurs*, which in Europe would have resulted in summary executions or imprisonment in extermination camps.

It may also be acknowledged that the work of pirates, corsairs and privateers has always carried with it a certain touch of glamour and romantic adventure which earned them an element of life-saving admiration.

3

Bligh of the Bounty

To be the victim of wild mutineers is shocking for any sea captain and is bound to arouse feelings of sympathy among the general public, especially when the victim and his few followers survived the evil deed and struggled half way across a vast ocean to eventual safety. It is hardly surprising, therefore, that over the centuries, the image of Captain Bligh has remained that of a hero whose fortitude in the face of a near disaster deserves admiration.

And there can be little doubt that his struggle and leadership after he was left in a small launch with 18 others to fend for himself and make his way from the small island of Tofua in the Tongan archipelago to Timor, a distance of over six thousand kilometres, which he achieved in 47 days, deserves recognition. William Bligh was a skilled navigator, a man whose career and background was closely associated with the British Royal Navy. When the news of the mutiny reached England, it was seen as a threat to the rulers of society and the safety of the country, for it had occurred in April 1789, while in France the Bastille had been captured by rioting revolutionaries in July of the same year. Both rebellious actions could be interpreted as warnings that the very safety of the state was under threat. Not surprisingly, the mutiny on the *Bounty* became the subject of numerous articles, books, poems and in time novels and films.

The mutineers were hunted down and their story similarly told and retold. But were they really traitors, or was William Bligh the brutal self-centred character they accused him of being?

He was born in what may be called an upper-middle-class family in 1754 and joined the navy as a ship's boy at the age of seven. This modest and fairly brief period of service enabled him to be accepted as an able seaman at the age of 16, then as a midshipman, rising to the rank of master's mate at the age of 21. He was highly regarded and well known among the younger officers, and had the good fortune to be selected by the great navigator James Cook to serve as master on the sloop *Resolution* for Cook's third and, tragically, last voyage to the Pacific. Cook's behaviour in the later part of the voyage may have contributed to the development of William Bligh's eventual brutality, for there were a number of occasions when Cook ordered brutal lashings with the dreaded cat-o'-nine-tails, which gave rise not only to cries of pain from his sailors, but also an attitude of surly behaviour that may well have contributed to James Cook's eventual death in Kealakekua Bay in Hawaii, where chaos reigned and orders were ignored. In general, it can be said that James Cook's character had worsened during this third voyage, and the young Bligh may have adopted his behaviour as a model.

When he returned to England, Bligh was able to provide details about Cook's death and naturally his own role during the expedition. He was upset, however, when his role in carrying out a number of surveys was largely ignored, and the leading personalities at the Admiralty and in the Royal Society took little notice of him. He had married shortly after his return to a pleasant and devoted wife, but the lack of credit he was given for his work meant that they lived in near poverty. He frequently expressed his indignation at what he considered ill-treatment by the upper classes, but fortunately for him the American War of Independence was in full swing, and he was able to return to the Royal Navy and take part in several naval engagements between the colonists and the British. The downside was that when the war ended in late 1781, Bligh found himself among the numerous officers affected by the widespread demobilisation that followed, and he had to return to the merchant navy. He finally succeeded in getting a commission

William Bligh

in August 1787 as "commanding lieutenant" in a small cutter, more grandly titled "H.M. Naval Vessel", bought from a firm of London-based merchants and renamed the *Bounty*. Its purpose was to collect breadfruit plants from Tahiti and other Pacific islands and take them to the West Indies where they would provide food for the growing number of slaves arriving there. Bligh was glad to be offered a chance to return to the navy, but displeased at his ranking – the lowest available, with no other officers to help him – but his complaints were ignored.

The *Bounty* was not an impressive vessel. It provided merely cramped quarters for the crew of just under 40 men, which included as mate the young Fletcher Christian with whom Bligh was acquainted and held in some regard. The expedition sailed from England in late December 1787, making its way to Tenerife and struggling through wild storms to eventually reach Tahiti. There had been a number of clashes between the men and Bligh, whose ability to cope with problems, including dealing with a shortage of food, was often inadequate, resulting in constant arguing and frequent floggings. The *Bounty* finally reached Tahiti in October 1788, and a stay of some five months began. The aim was to collect as many breadfruit plants as the small ship could carry, a task that was arduous and required careful negotiations with the islanders.

The stay was marked by sickness for some, relaxation and affairs with island women, and continuing arguments between Bligh, Fletcher Christian and other members of the crew. There were desertions, resulting in demotions and severe floggings when the culprits were brought back. When the *Bounty* finally set sail, there was a clear mood of depression and anger among the crew, led by Christian. Bligh sought to deal with this by threats, losing his temper on several occasions, and once accusing Christian of stealing some coconuts from his personal stock, for which he punished the entire crew by halving their food rations and stopping their meagre allocation of rum. The slightest complaint was met by Bligh's fury and threats of floggings, not always carried out. Christian and his supporters, deciding they could not bear to sail any further under Bligh, plotted the mutiny, which occurred on the morning of 28 April 1789. In the midst of shouting and cursing, Bligh and 18 loyal members of the crew were set adrift in the ship's launch, provided with roughly a week's supply of food and water, and left to begin their epic voyage to the Dutch East Indies. Fletcher Christian and his followers, plus a few loyalists who were unable to be accommodated on the small launch, had set sail for Tahiti, with some eventually making for other Pacific islands, including, more famously, the island of Pitcairn where the *Bounty* was scuttled so that the search party the navy was sure to send out in due course could not trace it.

When Bligh eventually made his way back to Britain, a court-martial was held to assess the affair of the *Bounty* and the causes of the mutiny and the loss of the ship. It was a normal procedure, which Bligh expected and for which he had prepared by drawing up lists of the crew's misdemeanours. He was exonerated, received his back pay and walked about with his head held high. However, a number of critics expressed their disapproval of his behaviour as commander of the *Bounty*, commenting on reports of his temper, his foul language and his inability to cope with the problems faced by his crew. Meanwhile, the Admiralty sent out a ship to hunt down the mutineers, the *Pandora*, which did succeed in

Captain Bligh is set loose from the HMS Bounty *as the mutineers make off with his ship.*

catching a number of the *Bounty*'s crew, including the unfortunate loyalists who had been left behind but were unable to prove their innocence. The *Pandora* sank off the Great Barrier Reef, and four of the mutineers, unable to escape from their cage-like prison, were drowned. The others were eventually sent to England to stand trial. Three of them ended their life on the gallows.

After his exoneration at the court-martial, Bligh was able to return to the Royal Navy, and undertook a second voyage to Tahiti to collect breadfruit for the West Indies. The expedition was far better planned than the *Bounty*'s had been: there were two ships, the *Providence* and the *Assistant*, coppered and well provisioned, and had the support of leading personalities, including the noted botanist Sir Joseph Banks and several religious leaders who were considering the need to Christianise the Pacific islands. They sailed on 2 August 1791 with the crew in good spirits, as most of what they had heard about Tahiti and the adjoining islands was that the people and especially the women were welcoming, and the climate was far more pleasant than England's. The first few months were peaceful, largely because Bligh was badly affected by malaria and kept most of the time to his own cabin. However, when his health improved, his ill-temper and shouting returned, causing the *Providence*'s first lieutenant, his own nephew, to complain of "his dictatorial attitude on trifles, and his everlasting fault-finding". His proud striding around the decks earned him the nickname of "Bligh the Don", an allusion to his tendency to act like a Spanish grandee. In general, however, the voyage was successful, the crew fully aware of Bligh's reputation as a quick-tempered commander, but the stay at Tahiti was marred by internal warring in the island, and they were glad to sail away and make for the West Indies, and finally to England where they arrived in August 1793.

By now, the trial of the few mutineers who had been caught was over, but opinion about William Bligh remained divided. The First Lord of the Admiralty, Lord Chatham, refused to see him, and critical accounts of the trial were being published. Nevertheless, as the war with France continued, so did Bligh's role in the navy, but mostly in British waters. While he was commander of the *Director*, mutinies occurred on several vessels, the sailors complaining, not without justification, about ill-treatment, lack of food and lack of pay. Sixteen ships were affected, including Bligh's *Director*, at the time anchored at the Nore near Sheerness. Brutal repression followed, with a total of 27 men being hanged and ten men from each ship being taken ashore to be flogged, imprisoned and eventually deported as convicts. Bligh, however, wisely seized the occasion to counter the allegations of cruelty and unfair treatment on board the *Bounty* by refusing to press any charges against any of his crew beyond the ten men declared to be activists on each ship.

The treaty of Amiens in 1802 brought about a temporary peace with France, and hostilities did not resume for a couple of years. Bligh went on half-pay for a while, but was successful in obtaining a new command in May 1804, that of the *Warrior*, an under-equipped 74-gun ship. Here, he fell out with the second lieutenant who had been put on the sick list by the ship's surgeon and asked for a discharge. Bligh shouted at him that this was disobedience and ordered him to be court-martialled. The lieutenant was exonerated and revenged himself by calling for Bligh to be court-martialled for ill-treatment of a sick officer and "tyrannical behaviour". Testimony was given of Bligh's foul language and physical ill-treatment. The Court acquitted Bligh of the more serious charges, but issued a formal reprimand against his general behaviour as a commander.

Shortly after this, Bligh's friends, led by Sir Joseph Banks, put forward a new proposal for his future: they suggested he be appointed commander of the newly founded colony of New South Wales in Australia. Not surprisingly, the young Australian settlements had been difficult to organise. The First Fleet had arrived less than 20 years earlier, in January 1788, bringing some 759 convicts, which included 191 women and 13 children, guarded by a couple of hundred marines and a handful of officers. The first governor, Arthur Phillip, found that Botany Bay offered too few facilities for a settlement, and he moved north to Port Jackson, where he founded a settlement he called Sydney, after Britain's Home Secretary. But he lacked skilled workers, such as carpenters and farmers, and in effect ran a prison camp. By 1792, when he gladly went back to Britain, a few farms had been established, but there were frequent clashes with the disgruntled Aboriginals, and the convicts, many of whom were in poor health, were reluctant to build a new colony for Britain. Food supplies came mostly from Norfolk Island, which also served as a kind of jail for the more difficult convicts.

The marines were replaced by new British recruits who formed what became known as the New South Wales Corps, and many of them turned into successful farmers and traders. They found a profitable outlet in buying and selling rum, avoiding paying any form of tax on it and defeating any attempt by successive short-term governors to put an end to it. It became almost a form of currency. New South Wales in effect lacked any administrative structure, including policing the growing corruption. Governor Phillip had been succeeded by Captain John Hunter who lasted a mere five years before being replaced by Captain Philip King who left in 1806, having been almost overthrown by a rebellion of Irish convicts. London authorities felt that William Bligh would be the firm hand that New South Wales needed if it was ever to be turned into a successful colony. They were aware that he had a short temper – his wife, who did not accompany him, wrote him a letter imploring him to be cautious and control his temper – but their main concern was the war in Europe and they believed that Bligh could cope in the meantime with the problems that might arise in that faraway country.

The situation required tact as well as firmness, but William Bligh soon showed that he entirely lacked any skill in dealing with others. When the Judge Advocate pointed out that a surgeon's suspension from office might be unlawful, he shouted back at him "Damn the law! My will is the law, and woe betide the man who dares to disobey me!" Soon afterwards, he said much the same thing to a powerful landowner, John Macarthur: "Damn the Privy Council! And damn the Secretary of State! What do they have to do with me?" He attempted to curb the power of the members of the Corps, had some properties knocked down and their land purchases cancelled. It was obvious to the settlers and the few appointed administrators that Bligh intended to rule by himself, as if indeed New South Wales was little more than a ship of which he was the sole captain. And as for the rum trade, he planned to abolish it entirely, and imprison or indeed hang any man who was shown to be trading illegally. Not surprisingly, when the anti-Bligh movement erupted it became known as the Rum Rebellion.

On 26 January 1808, some 400 soldiers of the New South Wales Corps marched on Government House and placed William Bligh under arrest. Some time later, a cartoon was drawn and circulated throughout the colony, showing Bligh hiding under his bed and being dragged out by a couple of soldiers, but it is unlikely that he gave up in so cowardly and so easy a manner. In spite of his protestations, undoubtedly yelled at the rebels, he was imprisoned in Government House, his reforms were overturned and he remained powerless until May 1809 when he was allowed to leave in the naval vessel *Porpoise*, but instead of sailing to England, as he had promised his captors, he went down to Tasmania, where he hoped to persuade the few colonists and officials in the new settlement of Hobart to join him in attacking the rebels in Sydney. He was largely ignored, none of the residents of Tasmania wanting to get involved in what might turn out to be a civil war. News soon came that a new governor, Lachlan Macquarie, was on his way to New South Wales, to replace Bligh and endeavour to reorganise the administrative structure overturned during the Rum Rebellion. Bligh accordingly sailed to Sydney to meet him and guide him in his new task, but once again his character proved this to be impossible, and the two men soon fell out, Macquarie commenting in a famous letter to his brother that "Bligh is certainly the most disagreeable person to have any dealings or public business to transact with; having no regard whatever to his promise or engagement, however sacred, and his natural temper is uncommonly harsh and tyrannical in the extreme".

Macquarie told him to keep the undertaking he had made to the locals when he was released from his home detention at Government House, and sail back to England. Bligh, largely ignored by the locals, could do little in Sydney, and he finally agreed to leave Australia and return to England, where he could plead his case and bear witness against any rebels who might be indicted. He arrived home in October and was soon embroiled in arguments about his actions in New South Wales and the charges that could be laid against his opponents. Opinion was largely divided, Bligh being mostly unpopular in Britain. He did not return to naval duties, but was promoted to rear-admiral and a little later vice-admiral, titles which soothed his temper and enabled him to live a few years in peaceful retirement. He died in London in December 1817, aged 63.

Villain or unlucky hero? William Bligh can be admired for his devotion to duty, his skill as a navigator, and as a dominant figure in Pacific history. But he had an ungovernable temper which spoiled his relations with almost every subordinate he dealt with and can be said to have ruined his life and the lives of many others. He entered the world of literature, even of poetry, although this was often tinged with sorrow, and of drama, cinema and television.

4

Mary Bryant and the Aftermath of the Bounty

Even in the late 18th century, thieves were commonly hanged, women included. The theft of a silk bonnet or a few lengths of cloth could easily lead to a public hanging. Such was the fate that awaited 23-year-old Mary Broad when she was caught stealing a bonnet in 1786. Fortunately for her, the judge was a merciful man and since plans were being made to establish a penal colony at a place called Botany Bay, somewhere down in Australia, she was given a sentence of seven years' forced labour, to be served abroad. Thus, mercy could be shown her, while England would be rid of another petty thief.

She knew nothing of New South Wales or that vast country at the other end of the world they called Australia. She lived in Fowey, a small Cornish port near St Austell, which as she boarded the convict ship the *Charlotte* in Portsmouth, she thought she would never see again. However, she would earn some fame, come what may, as one of the few women sent to Australia by the First Fleet. She spent some time in an English prison before the Fleet sailed in May 1787. It did not reach Botany Bay until January 1788. By then, she had had a child, whom she christened Charlotte.

It is evident that the child had been conceived while she was in prison, and it is likely that the father was a fellow convict, a smuggler named William Bryant, because she married him four days after landing on Australian soil. She may have known him in England, because he too came from a fishing village and may have been a Cornishman. His experience as a fisherman was useful in the new settlement, and he was soon put to work. However, conditions in the new colony were harsh in the extreme, and a number of convicts soon tried to escape. For the Bryants, the sea was the obvious escape route.

They had heard of the mutiny on board William Bligh's *Bounty* and that those few sailors who had remained faithful to Bligh had completed with him an amazing voyage of over 3,000 miles in a longboat and reached the island of Timor by way of Torres Strait.

A view of Botany Bay, New South Wales as the First Fleet arrived in January 1788, with Aboriginals in canoes witnessing the arrival.

They felt sure that they could do much the same thing, all the more so because their route would take them along the Australian coast, so that they would not have to cross a vast expanse of little-known seas, as Bligh had done. And furthermore, no English outposts had yet been established along the coast, and therefore there was no one to bar their way. They planned their escape very meticulously and were able to sneak away successfully on 28 March 1791, after three hard years in the penal settlement. A Dutchman, Detmer Smit, for whom they had done some work, had supplied them with a chart, a compass, two muskets and some food. It was a moonless night and none of the guards noticed them disappearing into the darkness – 11 of them: William and Mary Bryant and, by now, their two children, and seven other convicts. They managed to avoid the coral reefs, the currents and the occasional suspicious and unfriendly Aboriginals. They made their way along the coast, landing now and then on a deserted strip of land to get some fresh drinking water and some fruit. When they entered the Torres Strait, they found themselves being chased by some Aboriginals in canoes, and only a sudden squall came to their rescue by forcing their pursuers to turn back.

On 5 June 1791 they reached Kupang in Timor, the port where, just over two years earlier, Captain Bligh's longboat had landed with the 17 sailors who had supported him.

It was here that the story of Mary Bryant and of William Bligh intertwine. Bligh had managed to make it back to England, while after the mutiny Fletcher Christian had struggled to find a safe home somewhere in the vast Pacific. He had firstly returned to Tahiti which had proved to be such a pleasant and tempting world. Some of the mutineers were happy enough to stay there and enjoy the delights the island had offered. Fletcher Christian, however, felt that this was not a safe enough place. There were squabbles, at times deadly conflicts between rival groups of islanders, and he feared, rightly as it turned out, that Britain would send a ship or ships to seek and capture the men who had rebelled against Bligh.

He sailed off with nine others, plus six Tahitian men and twelve women, to look for a safer, less obvious place of refuge. The *Bounty* made her way south and east, and eventually settled on the steep, rocky and lonely island of Pitcairn which Philip Carteret in the *Swallow* had discovered in 1767. It was still uninhabited and so little known that Christian felt a search party would not bother to go there. To make sure that there would be no suspicion of their presence if any ship happened to sail past, he set fire to the *Bounty* and eliminated all traces of her landing. This also ensured that none of the mutineers or Tahitians could escape if they had second thoughts about becoming lifelong Pitcairners. They were discovered only by accident in 1808 by some passing whalers.

Meanwhile, the other mutineers who had remained in Tahiti, enjoying an easier and more exciting way of life, were to find that things could quickly turn sour. Fletcher Christian had been right in assuming that, once it learned about the rebellion on the *Bounty*, England would not take kindly to a mutiny on one of its naval ships which had been sent on an official expedition to collect breadfruit for its West Indian colonies. It took even less kindly to the way William Bligh, a naval officer who had sailed with the great James Cook, had been treated. When Bligh had finally reached London, the Admiralty had decided without delay to despatch a punitive expedition to arrest the mutineers. William Bligh may have been regarded by some as an unpleasant bully and an unpleasant captain, but he was a naval officer and the way he had been treated could certainly be condemned as an insult to a man of his rank. It chose for this a solid 24-gun three-master, the *Pandora*, which had recently served in the American War of Independence. It had a crew of 160 men and was commanded by Captain Edward Edwards, an experienced sailor who had just turned 50.

Sensibly the Admiralty drew up a double set of instructions. One was the capture and return to England of the *Bounty* mutineers, but the other was the completion of William Bligh's original mission by bringing back the thousand or so breadfruit seedlings he had collected. For this, the *Pandora* was provided with increased supplies of fresh water so that the plants could be regularly watered on their way to the West Indies. Realising that the *Pandora*'s voyage would be a long one, it was given additional supplies, including fishing tackle, fish hooks and fishing nets. But special provision was also made for the mutineers who were caught: the *Pandora* was eventually turned into the equivalent of a floating prison with the addition of the famous – or infamous – "Pandora's Box", a large metal cage some six metres long and three and a half metres wide set up on the main deck with a heavy metal bar fixed to the wooden deck. The prisoners were to be kept in this cage, their feet held in shackles attached to this bar. They would face a proper tribunal when they reached England, but meanwhile would be exposed to the sun or rain and unable to walk about at any time during the crossing to England. It was by no means an enviable fate.

The *Pandora* had sailed from Portsmouth on 7 November 1790, making for Tenerife, Rio de Janeiro and the Straits of Magellan. By an irony of fate, as the ship made her way across the Pacific, she sailed within a couple of hundred miles of Pitcairn Island, but as no one had any idea of what Fletcher Christian had actually done, Edwards blithely went on his way to Matavai Bay, in Tahiti. Wasting no time, he sent his men to look for the mutineers. He had the help of two of William Bligh's loyal supporters who had made their way back to England with him, and therefore knew that the mutineers had always been full of praise about the delights of Tahiti and had intended to make their way back there after getting rid of Bligh. And so, with surprisingly little delay, Edwards' men caught 14 of the mutineers. Only two were missing, killed in local inter-tribal conflicts. Not all of those arrested were mutineers, however: some had simply been unable to find room on Bligh's longboat when the mutiny had occurred and join the captain on his perilous journey. But Edwards took no notice of their pleas: they would have to argue their case when they faced the court-martials back in England. They were all locked into Pandora's Box which, unhappily for them, was large enough to accommodate all the prisoners, although in appalling conditions.

Captain Edwards then set about collecting breadfruit plants and setting them about in suitable parts of the ship. But meanwhile the crew had discovered that some of the prisoners, who had intended to settle down in Tahiti, had married into chiefly families. Six children had been born, and emotional scenes occurred when the wives realised their men were being taken away. One of them brought her baby on board, hoping to plead for the captain's mercy. Her husband, broken-hearted, asked the sailors not to allow her to come to him, knowing that Edwards was as inflexible and as pitiless as Bligh himself would have been. The woman is said to have died not long after the *Pandora's* departure. Such scenes affected the Polynesians, who were not only moved by the sorrowful scenes they were witnessing, but also felt insulted by the Englishman's actions in breaking up what were legal local marriages, mostly to women of rank. They decided to cut the *Pandora's* cables, so that the ship might drift ashore and end up on the reefs, but Edwards heard about the plot and promptly broke off all contact with the shore. He had caught a number of mutineers and collected a goodly number of plants, and he felt it wiser to set sail.

His major concern was to catch Fletcher Christian. There was no sign of him on Tahiti, nor of the *Bounty*, and the prisoners confirmed that the leader of the mutineers had sailed away in the *Bounty*. So Edwards set out to look for him and for the missing ship, sailing for three months among the Pacific islands, going as far as Fiji and Tonga. There was no sign of him anywhere, as Christian had taken good care not to tell anyone he left behind where he planned to go. Captain Edwards decided he could waste no more time on this search: he still faced a journey of 15,000 kilometres to take the *Pandora* and her prisoners back to Portsmouth. He decided to start for home, passing through the Endeavour Channel which James Cook had sailed along 20 years earlier. This meant finding his way along and through the Great Barrier Reef off the coast of Queensland, about which still very little was known. During the night of 29 August 1791, just as the men in the boat he had sent along to take soundings shouted that they had found a pass, a strong current drove the *Pandora* onto the reef. Water poured into the hold. With the help of a few prisoners whose shackles had been broken, the sailors rushed to man the pumps. However, noticing that some of the prisoners had freed themselves, Captains Edwards ordered some of the soldiers to keep watch over the others and shoot any who might try to escape.

Despite all their desperate efforts, the crew and their helpers were unable to save the ship which slowly continued to sink. At daybreak, the men were told to jump into the boats. Edwards was the last man on board; he then jumped off and swam to one of the boats. But although he was praised as the last to stay on board, there were still prisoners caught in Pandora's Box. The sailor who held the keys threw them to the men at the last minute, so that those who were still handcuffed or shackled could free themselves. One of the ship's boys, a youth named William Moulter, went back to help them, but for four of them it was all too late: the ship was sinking and the waves were beginning to splash over the cage. In all, four mutineers and 31 sailors and soldiers perished in the wreck of the *Pandora*.

The survivors gathered on a small sandy islet and after a brief period of rest began to get organised for a difficult voyage to what was the most promising port, Kupang in the Dutch East Indies. They were allocated to the various small boats, sailors and soldiers and two or three mutineers, some still in handcuffs. They all endured the heat and growing pangs of hunger and thirst before finally reaching Kupang in September 1791. When they arrived, Hayward and Hallett, the two men who had been part of Captain Bligh's original crew and who had survived with him in the longboat, introduced themselves to the governor, Timothy Wairyou or Wanjon, and received the same kind welcome as when they had struggled into Kupang on the earlier unhappy occasion.

Meanwhile, over the previous three months, Mary Bryant, with her family and friends, had been enjoying the same Dutch hospitality. The story they told was that they were survivors from the wreck of a whaling ship. The kindly governor believed them, and they were provided with fresh clothing, food and lodgings. The problem was that William Bryant was a little too fond of his drink and became dangerously talkative and quarrelsome when he was drunk. He argued loudly with the other English convicts; they were overheard and when the governor realised that they were nothing more than escaped convicts, he had them arrested. He was still wondering how he might get rid of them when Captain Edwards struggled into harbour with his motley crew of survivors.

Waryou was delighted and handed Mary Bryant and her friends over to him. Edwards treated the Bryants and their friends just like the ten surviving mutineers he had caught in Tahiti. He arranged a passage to Batavia for everyone on a Dutch East Indies Company ship, the *Rembang*, placing all the prisoners, with the exception of Mary Bryant, in shackles down in the hold. Once in Batavia, Edwards arranged for all of them to be kept in a jail.

Mary Bryant's misfortunes continued, with the death of her son, then of her husband, both victims of the fevers that so often affected Europeans travelling through Java. She did not blame William Bryant altogether for their misfortunes, because even if he had not been so careless, Captain Edwards would eventually have put two and two together and "invited" them to accompany him to Portsmouth.

Inflexible, Captain Edwards found a ship, the *Horsen*, which could take them all to the Cape of Good Hope. At this point, one of the prisoners, Jonathan Cox, the chief helper in William Bryant's escape plan and a fisherman like him, threw himself overboard. He had no wish to face the hangman he felt awaited him in England. When they reached the Cape, Captain Edwards transferred his prisoners to a warship. And it was then that Mary Bryant's second child died. Little Charlotte was five; she was born on a ship and she died on a ship. Finally, on 18 June 1792, HMS *Gorgon*, a well-named naval vessel, dropped anchor off Portsmouth, the port Mary had left five years earlier. Captain Edwards had completed his task. The prisoners he brought back were separated: the Botany Bay convicts, Mary Bryant and her party, were taken to London and appeared before a civilian court, while the *Bounty* mutineers who, in spite of their style of dress, were still part of the navy, were brought before a court-martial.

At the Old Bailey, the judges were not unsympathetic towards the escaped convicts who had undergone such hardships, but they were not prepared to create any precedents and pardon them. However, they were not too ruthless. Mary Bryant thought she might have to serve another seven years with hard labour and probably be returned to Australia; most of the others expected to be hanged. They all received prison terms, Mary being sentenced to a year in Newgate Prison, but luck favoured her. Her story was so extraordinary, she had suffered so much during the previous five years, and the original crime for which she had been deported was, after all, not that serious. People began to talk about her, and the famous writer and lawyer James Boswell decided to take up her cause. A man of influence, with friends at court, he pleaded her case so that she was finally pardoned in May 1793, having already spent ten months in prison. The authorities' clemency even extended to the other surviving escaped convicts, one of whom later joined the army and went back to New South Wales wearing the king's uniform. Mary returned to Fowey, to spend the rest of her life in peace and quiet and welcome obscurity. She was fortunate enough to avoid the penury that probably awaited her because Boswell paid her a pension of ten pounds a year. And in time, she entered Australia's folklore and even became the subject of a television play.

The *Bounty* mutineers were less fortunate. They had no Boswell to plead their case. Quite the opposite: Captain Bligh who had sailed to Tahiti to complete the task of collecting breadfruit plants had left behind a report on the behaviour and the level of guilt of each of the prisoners. The court-martial, guided by this, acquitted four of the men but sentenced the other six to death by hanging. Three death sentences were later commuted to life imprisonment. The other three men were hanged in October 1792, thus ending one of the most famous mutinies in history.

5

Mutinous Mutineers

*L*ife on board the old merchantmen and whalers was hard and often dreary. To keep the crew under control required a firm hand, but all too often the captain and his few mates allowed mere strictness to turn into oppression and brutality. The usual consequence was desertions at some distant port, whereupon if the men were not caught and dragged back to further punishment they had to be replaced by unemployed locals, some of whom at times turned out to have been deserters from some other ship.

Mutineering, however, was far more serious a crime than desertion. It was a fairly rare occurrence, usually the result of constant brutality or of a total lack of sympathy or understanding on the part of the captain or his associates. It occurred among pirates in such areas as the Caribbean, but even there it was relatively rare because the captains or leaders were themselves strong and watchful, ready to defend themselves whenever danger threatened. In the largely unexplored world of the Pacific Ocean, mutineers were kept in check by a fear of the unknown, and mutinies were infrequent.

An early and much discussed mutiny occurred in 1824 on the whaling ship *Globe* which had sailed from its base at Nantucket, near New York, on 22 December 1822. Whaling was a profitable endeavour, each whale caught yielding fat, known as blubber, that was boiled down into oil, for which there was a steady market. The *Globe* was owned by merchants from Nantucket and had sailed on several occasions since the mid-1810s. Reports that there were whales in large numbers to be found in Pacific waters decided the owners to send the *Globe* on a mission to the Pacific Ocean under an experienced captain, Thomas Worth, with a trusted first mate by the name of William Beetle. Among the total complement of 21 men was one who later became famous, Samuel B. Comstock, a 22-year-old steerer and harpooner, and his younger brother George who joined the crew as a ship's boy.

Although Comstock has been accused of plotting right from the start to take over the ship, and been condemned by public opinion as a crooked and ambitious man, this seems unlikely as nothing serious occurred for over a year. The *Globe* sailed down to the Cape Verde Islands, west of Africa, then down to the Falkland Islands, rounded Cape Horn into the Pacific and continued north towards the Hawaiian Islands. The expedition seems to have caught only one whale during the early part of the voyage, which could indicate that whale numbers were well down in Atlantic waters by then or, more probably, that Captain Worth's mission was to go whaling in the Pacific area, and not waste his time hunting through well-known seas. In Hawaii, he replenished his dwindling stock of provisions and sailed off to what were referred to as the Japan Seas. His whaling endeavours here were most successful, with enough whales caught to produce over 500 barrels of oil. At this point, the *Globe* sailed back to Oahu, one of the Hawaiian Islands, to obtain further supplies, continue its whale hunting and sail for home.

It was at this time that the troubles that had been developing among the crew came to the surface and six men deserted while in Hawaii. There had been complaints about inadequate food rations, the food itself being often inedible, about severe and foul-mouthed reprimands by the captain and his mates for the slightest of errors, often accompanied by punching and slappings and at least one severe public flogging. Worth attempted to find the deserters, but they had easily disappeared in the island bush. He managed to find replacements for them from the few Britons or Americans living on the island, either deserters from another ship or men who had decided to try their luck among the Hawaiians. He then sailed south, still looking for the odd whales, but essentially making his way towards Cape Horn, planning to return to Nantucket.

On the way, he stopped at Fanning Island, part of a group some 900 miles south of Oahu. And there occurred the mutiny for which the *Globe* became famous, frightening a number of other trading or whaling captains in Pacific waters. It was 26 January 1824. Samuel Comstock crept up to the captain who was asleep in his hammock and killed him with one of the large knives used to cut through the whales. The three mates, William Beetle, John Lumbert and Nathaniel Fisher, were similarly despatched, and the four bodies were unceremoniously thrown overboard. Four of the men who had been taken on at Oahu played a major role in the mutiny – Silas Payne, John Oliver, William Humphries and Joseph Thomas – an indication that their presence in the Hawaiian Islands was due to insubordination and unruly behaviour on other vessels. Comstock took over the role of captain, drew up a set of rules and sailed west towards the central Pacific, since it would have been disastrous to make for Valparaiso or some other American port as the authorities would immediately arrest the mutineers and execute them for murder.

He soon discovered, however, that controlling mutineers was no easy task. It came to light that one of the men they had taken on in Hawaii was plotting to take over command. This man, William Humphries, had proved to be troublesome soon after the mutiny, and Comstock suspected that others were plotting with him. He arranged a formal trial, accusing Humphries of planning his own mutiny. Humphries was hanged after a vote had been taken among the crew on whether he was guilty or not: Comstock intended to show that some form of democracy and unity could be developed and that the traditional brutality of ships' commanders could be avoided. He also realised that, since the mutineers could not make for a port where European or American authorities might be in charge, their future lay in some little-known Pacific island where they might safely settle, and he would become the ruler. It was not, however, something he seems to have discussed with most of the crew. They were satisfied that Humphries deserved his fate, as there had been whispers of his intention to start a mutiny against Comstock, and that he was a worthless character as some of the captain's belongings, which he had stolen, including 16 dollars in

Whaleman Samuel Comstock despatches ship's mate John Lumbert during the mutiny on the Globe.

coin, were found hidden in his bunk. For a while Comstock merely carried on as captain, endeavouring to earn the respect of the men until something worthwhile eventuated.

The *Globe* sailed cautiously to Kingsmill Island, formerly called the Gilbert Islands and currently Kiribati, where they obtained fresh food, and then to the Marshall Islands. Comstock and his followers were looking for some island where they might settle, but meanwhile bought coconuts and breadfruit from the islanders. The problem was that the islanders, although willing to trade, were often unfriendly, hurling stones and rough weapons at the strange white-skinned aliens who were trying to come ashore in a ship's boat. In mid-February 1824, the *Globe* reached Mili Atoll, a group of some 92 small islands and reefs, part of the Marshall Islands, but scarcely known at the time. It was to become better known in the 19th century, believed to have been the area where Amelia Earhart's plane was lost, and a site for naval and aircraft combat during the Second World War.

The men of the *Globe* were able to obtain more supplies from the few locals they saw, who seemed more friendly than other islanders they had met. Comstock told his men that he had decided to anchor off the atoll and stay there for a few days, but Silas Payne, another of the men taken on in the Hawaiian Islands, became suspicious where he saw Comstock and several others ferrying supplies and equipment ashore. It does seem clear that, at this point, Comstock was planning to settle on the atoll and destroy evidence of the mutiny by hauling the ship ashore and burning it down. The atoll, with its 200 to 300 inhabitants, could hardly support all the crewmen, and the life which Comstock envisaged for himself and a few others was not appealing to all. A shouting match began; Silas Payne and a fellow crewman from Hawaii, John

Oliver, then carried out a counter-mutiny, killing Comstock and trying to take over command.

Payne and Oliver felt that Comstock's plan to settle on the Milis was viable, and decided to continue unloading equipment and other supplies from the ship. They sent Gilbert Smith to the *Globe* to organise the operation, since he was the most senior survivor of the original mutiny, a steersman who knew his way about the ship, including any hiding holes where tools or other items might have been concealed by Worth or Comstock. But this was a mistake: Smith and several others were afraid of Silas Payne and his plans, and also of eventually being caught and accused of being mutineers and murderers. They cut the ropes at night and managed to sneak away and make their way to Valparaiso, where they arrived in June 1824.

They were arrested by the American consul, and tried for mutiny, but treated with sympathy. The *Globe* was taken over by a Captain King, who sailed her back to Nantucket, where she anchored in late November.

Meanwhile, on the islands, Silas Payne and his supporters had endeavoured to form a settlement, but the islanders, not surprisingly, were reluctant to be ordered about by the strange white men, told to supply them with food and to help in building tents and huts. Several attacks took place, the mutineers began to run out of gunpowder and ammunition, and finally all except two were killed. The two survivors, Cyrus Hussey and William Lay, were taken by two sets of villagers, and attempted to help the locals by teaching them white men's practices, such as knot tying and even fishing. They were carefully kept away from each other, so that they could not plot against their new masters.

They lived a lonely life, always fearful of what might happen to them, until late December 1825 when a ship appeared, the US schooner *Dolphin*, which had been sent to search for survivors. Hussey and Lay managed to sneak on board, in spite of the islanders' attempts to hold them back, but the American captain avoided any unpleasantness by giving the islanders a quantity of presents, expressing his thanks through Hussey who had managed to learn some of the local dialect and could act as interpreter, for their good treatment of the survivors. This done, they sailed to Valparaiso, calling on the way at the Hawaiian Islands, and handing Hussey and Lay over to the authorities.

The two men were naturally examined by these authorities, but it was recognised that they had not actively participated in the mutiny and that they had suffered enough from the tragedy of the *Globe*. They were transferred to the frigate *United States*, which sailed on several missions to Peru and elsewhere, then to the *Brandywine*, which was on her way back to the United States, by way of Cape Horn, where they arrived in late April 1827. They found there was much public interest both in the mutinies that had occurred on the *Globe* and in their own life among the islanders. There had been a great deal of talk among whalers and the residents of their home district. Hussey, in particular, was invited to give talks to various groups, and together with Lay wrote a book entitled *A Narrative of the Mutiny, on board the ship* Globe, *of Nantucket, in the Pacific Ocean*, which included details of their two years' stay on the isolated atoll. It was published in New London, in Connecticut, in 1828, and was widely read. Both men enjoyed a successful life after this, Hussey becoming a figure of note in the Nantucket district.

6

William Hayes: Bully and Thief

For years, William Henry Hayes has been known as "Bully Hayes", a buccaneer or pirate of the South Seas, an imposing personality, a man who travelled through the Pacific, inspiring both fear and admiration. To call him a pirate, however, is a misnomer, largely a creation of journalists who referred to him in articles as "the last of the pirates" and of authors such as the Australian Rolf Boldrewood who published a biography in 1894 entitled *A Modern Buccaneer*, and Will Lawson whose *The Laughing Buccaneer* appeared in 1935. Piracy involves searching the seas for passing vessels, attacking them, killing most of the crews and sinking the ships. It gives an image of bloodthirsty robbers waving swords and, even more dramatically, flying the skull and cross-bones. Hayes was more simply a confidence trickster and a thief, although admittedly he was also a recklessly brutal individual.

He was born in America, probably in Cleveland, Ohio, around the year 1828. He is understood to have joined the United States Navy and served in the China Station. He then left it, resigning his post or, as some have claimed, being court-martialled and sacked for having hanged some Chinese pirates without bothering to hold

The only known photograph of William Henry "Bully" Hayes.

a trial. Whether this is true or not, he is reported as having sailed as a trader or smuggler in the China seas, going down with various cargoes as far as Singapore. Not surprisingly, the details of his activities are vague and often contradictory, but he seems to have taken part in opium smuggling and the so-called coolie trade, by which Chinese labourers, poverty-stricken and unemployed, were taken from China, usually from the port of Swatow (Shantou) north-east of Canton, and delivered to railway construction sites or plantations in such places as Malaya, with practically no chance of ever returning home or finding ways of settling down. This was not unlike the later "blackbirding" trade, which dealt in a similar way with Pacific islanders.

Travelling through eastern ports, he made visits to traders and residents, looking for opportunities to make money and impressing people by his appearance and ease of manner. Years later, an old seaman who had sailed with him from Hong Kong to Australia described him in the *Akaroa Mail* newspaper as "a fine-looking man, over six feet in height, and built proportionally. He had an aquiline nose and light blue eyes that seemed to penetrate one when he looked at you, and long black hair". But the seaman also recalled how brutal Hayes could be, hitting his crewmen if they argued or misbehaved, and even on one occasion breaking the helmsman's arm. This brings up the issue of the term "Bully" about which writers have puzzled over the years. The term *bulli* is found in the language of Samoa, meaning "evasive", and is believed to have been used by the Reverend Rabone, a missionary in the islands, to refer to Captain Hayes' unreliability. Both interpretations can be accepted, for William Hayes could be both brutal and charming whenever he planned to cheat someone he met.

His practice of buying goods and cargo on credit, failing to pay for them, and then declaring temporary bankruptcy is outlined in a newspaper report published in Singapore in November 1856. He had incurred debts on a previous voyage but "his reappearance renewed confidence among our tradesmen as to his honesty, and the admirable nonchalance with which he comported himself enabled him to make extensive additions to the large sums which he already owed… He named a day on which he intended to leave the harbour, and requested that his creditors should send their agent on board for the repayment of their respective accounts at a certain hour of the day in question". He was well received, explained that circumstances had prevented him from paying on time for his previous purchases, but that everything was now under control. Naturally, by the day in question, he had sailed away, leaving all his debts behind, including a mortgage on his ship.

He was on his way to Java, in the Dutch East Indies, where he incurred more debts, then sailed away to Australia. He spent most of 1857 sailing to various ports, incurring debts and carrying passengers, many of whom were convicts on parole who were trying to escape from the localities where they had been doing forced labour. He also married a widow named Amelia Littleton from Adelaide. He had already had several affairs, reportedly one with a

Chinese woman, one with a barmaid from Adelaide, and one with the daughter of the Fremantle harbour-master, but none of them had lasted. Nor did his marriage. Amelia left him in Honolulu less than two years later and applied for a divorce on the grounds of ill-treatment. Hayes later lived in New Zealand with a member of a family of actors, a woman named Rosa Buckingham who called herself "Mrs Hayes", until she was drowned in a boating accident near Nelson. Then in 1865 he married again, a New Zealand hotel worker named Emily Butler. Whether his divorce had come through or whether he had other affairs is not clear. Hayes was known for the many differing versions he gave of his adventures and misadventures, depending on whether he was seeking to impress his listeners or simply confuse them. It is not surprising that in 1869 a farce was presented at the Adelphi Theatre in Sydney, entitled "Captain Hayes, the Husband of Many Wives".

His marriage to Amelia Littleton had soon encountered problems associated with his activities as a fraudster. The various merchants who had been fooled into granting him credit had naturally found it hard to trace his whereabouts and warn others in different ports, as the means of communication in the mid-19th century were slow and unreliable, but eventually they traced him to Australia and started proceedings. Bully Hayes dealt with the problem by filing for bankruptcy. This meant that legal proceedings could begin their slow process while the lawyers collected the necessary evidence. But when the first court sitting was held in March 1858, Bully Hayes had disappeared, and the case floundered as he pursued his shady dealings in other parts of the South Seas.

Hayes had gone to Honolulu, having first sailed to Melbourne to obtain a new command. In Hawaii, he went about in his usual manner, running up bills, buying supplies on credit and engaging in shady dealings which resulted in an attempt by the authorities to place him under arrest. He evaded this in his usual style, fooling the sheriff who came aboard to get him, and sailed on towards California. By then, his wife had left him, threatening to sue him for his violent behaviour. A bully he certainly was by nature, but she no doubt also had to put up with his drinking, for which he was renowned, and which worsened his temper. Ironically, when Bully Hayes became a figure of South Seas fiction, "Bully Hayes Rum", a drink that was named after him, became quite popular.

After some shady dealings along the coast of California, the details of which are naturally vague and often contradictory, seeing Bully Hayes' usual unreliability and his noted ability to confuse anyone he dealt with, he appears to have sailed towards Samoa in the brig *Ellenita* which sank in Samoan waters in November or December 1859. Some of the passengers struggled to find land in a makeshift raft, while Hayes and a few others made their way to Apia in the ship's boat. He then got a passage to Australia. Carefully avoiding Adelaide where he was known as a bankrupt, he went to Sydney. However, in Apia, he had borrowed money from a gullible fellow captain, claiming that he owned a ship the man could take over. This led to charges of fraud, but Hayes once again filed for bankruptcy. While local lawyers sorted out the appropriate papers, he sailed away, looking for more opportunities in the Dutch East Indies, then back to Australia.

By now, his reputation had become known to too many people for him to continue his practice of sailing to a major port, charming or threatening the people and running off with cargo he had not paid for. It was now 1862 and he decided to try his luck in New Zealand where gold had recently been found. He had obtained the command of a barque, the *Cincinnati*, and offered "unrivalled accommodation for passengers", as his advertisement put it, to the Otago goldfields. It seems that he left behind several people who had paid their fare, but he did take with him a family of actors, the Buckinghams, who had been working in Australia, but who were now keen to try their luck in New Zealand.

The Buckinghams arrived in Dunedin in September, after a rather uncomfortable crossing. Bully Hayes had apparently done some work with them in Australia, and he now decided to sell the *Cincinnati* and join the Buckinghams as their manager and part actor.

They gave two concerts in Dunedin, but were not particularly successful. There were other, better known companies in Dunedin: Mrs Foley, a famous melodrama and Shakespearean actress, was advertising "Select Drawing Room Entertainments" from her vast repertoire; while for those who preferred a more popular form of entertainment there was a troupe known as the San Francisco Minstrels. Hayes decided to take the Buckinghams to the goldfields, where there was no competition and audiences were less demanding. They presented their show in Dunstan at the United States Hotel, a rather grand title for what was little more than a canvas-covered grog shop. The audiences enjoyed the songs, but also enjoyed listening to Bully Hayes. He kept them enthralled with his yarns about the South Seas and his stories of cannibals and dusky maidens, and often laughed when he offered to take the gold-miners with him on his next voyage. He would often climb up on a table and sing or merely talk, throwing back his head with loud guffaws of laughter. It was not the performance a professional stage manager would have wanted, or the orderly programme Dunedin audiences would have expected, but here, among the rough miners, holding their tankards of beer or rum, he was a great success over the Christmas and New Year periods.

They then went on to a new settlement soon to be known as Arrowtown, where they built a rather rough structure of sod and timber, which they grandly named the Prince of Wales Hotel and Theatre. The Buckinghams were beginning to tire of Bully Hayes and his domineering manner, and they set up a rival establishment, the Provincial Hotel. However, one of the family, Rosa Buckingham, had become pregnant by him, and they were married – or at least she became known as Mrs William Hayes. Their rivalry produced some entertaining theatre for the locals: claiming that Bully Hayes' abundant hair was specially cut to hide the fact that he had lost an ear in a fight some years back when his opponent had claimed he was cheating at poker, the Buckinghams produced a farce entitled "The Barbarous Barber", in which a barber is bribed to cut a man's hair in such a way as to reveal the fact that he lacks one ear. This resulted in a great deal of abuse being shouted at the actors and their supporters, but made sure that the Buckinghams enjoyed large audiences. Spectators went to see Bully Hayes' shows in equally large numbers, but no one was bold enough to check whether the tales were based on fact: who but a man tired of life would dare pull a pirate's hair?

It soon became time for Hayes to move on. A storm had damaged his grog shop and theatre, and his old habit of running up bills without ever paying them off was too strong for him to resist. He vanished from Arrowtown and went down with Rosa to Riverton, near Invercargill in the south, running up a few more bills, then sailed back to Australia with her and her brother George, leaving behind the usual unpaid bills. His swift reconciliation with members of the Buckingham family suggests that the bitter arguments over the missing ear might have been little more than a cunning scheme devised by Hayes and the Buckinghams to fill their respective ramshackle theatres.

He soon found himself in difficulties in Sydney and later in Brisbane, having run up more bills and having to cope with creditors from earlier times who began to sue him. He managed to buy a small ship in Sydney, the *Black Diamond*, and slipped out of the harbour with his unpaid cargo before a formal complaint could be laid. He had apparently planned to sail to the South Seas to sell his cargo and do a little trading, but he first needed to refit his ship and so sailed to New Zealand, carefully avoiding the gold-fields and southern region where he had incurred such massive debts. Instead, in August 1864, he made for Croisilles Harbour, a short distance from Nelson. And there tragedy struck: his wife and her young child, as well as George Buckingham, were drowned in a boating accident which Bully Hayes only just survived. Some claims were made that this was no mere accident, but had been engineered by Hayes himself because he had tired of his marriage, but this may be a fabrication of his numerous enemies. Whatever the truth of this may be, it spelt disaster for Hayes, because the publicity the incident received drew attention to his presence, and his many creditors organised themselves to reclaim his brigantine and its cargo.

They knew all too well that he would now try to sneak away, so the Nelson agent of the man who had sold Hayes the *Black Diamond* and had never received a penny for it rowed out to it at night with a party of armed men and seized the ship while Bully Hayes was still asleep. Hayes woke up, shouted at the men and threatened them with an axe, but he was overpowered, and the vessel was seized and eventually sold. Hayes was also sued by crewmen for unpaid wages, but claimed he was himself penniless and fled Nelson to rejoin survivors of the Buckingham family down in Christchurch.

He spent the following year doing some acting – rough comedy turns in hotels in most cases – and taking occasional trading trips around New Zealand and apparently to Fiji. Then on 26 July 1865, less than a year after Rosa's tragic death, Hayes married again, this time to Emily Butler, a young barmaid from Christchurch.

It was as colourful an event as he could make it. He presented the people of Christchurch with the picture of a repentant troublemaker, a former pirate, but now a sorrowful widower being consoled by the love of a kind, good woman. He admitted that he had once been unreliable and something of a wild and sometimes dishonest entertainer in the goldfields, but now they would see him settling down to a new life. Some held on to their wallets and made sure they did not grant him any credit, but others took a kinder view and agreed to support him morally and to some extent financially – to help Captain Hayes build up a new life for himself and his young wife and contribute to the development of the province of Canterbury . . . Then, bills unpaid as usual, he vanished, going back to shady trading in the Pacific islands and leaving more gullible dealers out of pocket.

In May 1866, he was sailing in the *Rona,* going to Rarotonga, Samoa, the Fijis and other islands, carrying cargo for which he sometimes paid, but usually sailed off with little more than a promise to return and settle his bills once he had sold the goods. He also occasionally carried off island labourers to be delivered to planters in various islands, thus taking part in the infamous blackbirding trade. Reports of his whereabouts were seldom correct and never precise, but it is known that the *Rona* was wrecked in May 1869 somewhere off the island of Manihiki, in the Cook Islands. Bully Hayes took over another small schooner, the *Atlantic*, and made his way to Samoa, where he was arrested for his blackbirding activities.

He naturally made counter-claims, delaying the proceedings which were to involve his being sent to Sydney for a formal trial. And when the opportunity presented itself, he simply vanished. It was now 1870 and as news travelled slowly in the days of sailing ships the authorities were often confused over his whereabouts. He seems to have obtained a new ship and carried on his blackbirding activities, combined with trading and carrying the occasional passenger. However, by mid-1872, the Pacific Islanders Protection Act had been passed by the British government to put an end to the blackbirding trade, and the USS *Narragansett* finally caught up with Hayes in Apia. The evidence was insufficient to hold him, and he continued his shady dealings, avoiding, though any blatant trading and keeping clear of the increasing number of warships, American and British, which were at work clearing the seas of undesirables, among whom he now figured prominently.

The Spanish authorities were equally eager to get rid of men like him, and in late 1874 he was arrested and taken to Manila on various charges, including smuggling out Spanish prisoners and brutality towards his own crew. As usual, he claimed he was innocent or misled, assured his captors that he was a faithful Catholic, attended church services and used all his acting talents to fool them. Then, as usual, he vanished.

His luck ended in March 1877 in the Marshall Islands. He had bought the schooner *Lotus* and among his small crew was a Norwegian sailor who also served as cook. Hayes beat him for some error he had committed while at the helm, then lost his temper and shouted that he was going to get his revolver and shoot him. He went below deck, and as he came up, the man beat him with an iron bar and killed him. His body was thrown overboard, and the culprit successfully pleaded self-defence. So ended the life of a man who had ill-treated and swindled thousands of people, but had also entertained many and created a personality that would endure.

He had been talked about for years and many newspaper articles had been written about him. He continued to be the subject of articles and published reminiscences after his death, and his rough, brutish personality was transformed into something of a heroic figure, a man of great skills, even though the background against which this semi-fictional character appeared was clearly one of theft, roguery and viciousness. Not only are there books that enshrine him as a major figure in the history of the South Seas, but he also has his own enjoyable memorial in Akaroa, The Bully Hayes Restaurant and Bar.

7

Captain Bureau, Unlucky Trader

The Pacific world offered many opportunities to anyone bold enough to sail into its waters – or at least that is what many sailors and merchants believed as they listened to the stories that were being told in ports and inns. Emile Bureau was a man who came from Nantes in western France, and who had good links with the seaman's world. He went off to America, working on ships and eventually trading on his own. At some time in 1834 he had made his way to Valparaiso, in Chile, where he heard a great deal about the money that could be made by trading simple beads, old items of clothing, and even weapons in exchange for tortoise shells, trepangs or sea-slugs also known as bêche-de-mer, sandalwood, pearls and other items that could be sold in China or elsewhere at a good profit.

The American Benjamin Vanderford, from Massachusetts, had been one of the first to discover the money that could be made from buying bêche-de-mer, having sailed along the coasts of Viti Levu and other Fijian islands in 1822 to 1827, and using the services of a local beachcomber, a man named Whippy, who acted as an interpreter and negotiator with the local chiefs. The profits he made out of his dealings were still the talk of the early 1830s when Bureau arrived in America, looking for opportunities to trade or carry cargo among the islands of the Pacific and on the developing trade route between Asia and the Americas.

There were, however, reports that sailing among the islands and dealing with the inhabitants, although profitable, could be a dangerous endeavour, and the Americans, when they heard of Bureau's plans, wrote warning him of the risks he would be taking. Bureau did not worry too much about this, intent on first obtaining the help of Fijians and Melanesians in the islands he intended to visit. This, he believed, would save him from the fate that had befallen other traders, whose often tragic end was a frequent topic among those who discussed the changing Pacific Ocean world.

He heard, among other tales, about the trader *Glide* which had been attacked on three occasions in 1830, but had fortunately been pre-warned by one of the beachcombers. In July 1830, the American vessel *Peru* was similarly targeted by one group of Fijians, but was also fortunate enough to discover the plot before it was too late, and called back the men who had gone ashore to negotiate with the islanders. It went on to trade cautiously elsewhere, but the outcome was a fierce war that developed between the men of Rewa and those of Bau, each accusing the other of betraying their plans to the Americans.

In 1833, the *Charles Doggett*, under Captain Batchelder, was anchored at Ono Island, south of Suva, when it discovered a plot to haul the ship close to the shore during the night, preventing it from moving when it was attacked in the morning. It changed its location, following the advice of the beachcomber whose services the captain was using, a man named Paddy Connell, believed to be an escaped convict from Australia. Batchelder, however, did not discover another plot, which resulted in his second-in-command, nine sailors and two Tahitian helpers being attacked and killed. This time, Batchelder fired his guns against the raiders, and eventually succeeded in negotiating the return of the bodies, saving them from being cooked and eaten, a fate that had already befallen one of the Tahitians. The dead were sewn into sheets and buried at sea but, so they learnt later, the ceremony was being watched by the islanders who recovered the bodies and cooked them – as they had intended to do all along.

Added to these gory tales were narratives of attacks carried out against the Spanish traders who at times had recruited Filipinos known as the Manila Men. They were useful because of their knowledge of the islands and the trade routes, but were often unreliable and given to theft and attempts at piracy. In 1825, the brig *Laurice* had taken on board more than the usual maximum of five of these Manila Men, with the result that, once out of sight of land, they attacked the captain and the few Spanish crew members, took over the ship and started trading on their own among the Fiji islands. The Spanish authorities, based in the Philippines, took care to warn other traders and tried as best they could to supervise their recruiting of local crew members, but this did not prevent other attempts at betrayal, with the Manila Men secretly negotiating with the islanders they met and helping them on a number of occasions to attack a party coming ashore or to creep up to a ship at anchor during the night.

Bureau was confident he could avoid these perils, having purchased a small former warship, which he renamed the *Aimable Josephine*, after the trading brig he had brought to Valparaiso. Captain Eagleston, who had commanded the *Peru* during its earlier voyage and was now in charge of the *Emerald*, wrote to him, warning him about the dangers he might have to face. Bureau, however, ignored his advice, putting it down to mere jealousy. A further warning came in the form of the resignation of two American sailors he had taken on in Tahiti, who refused to undertake a voyage they now realised would be too dangerous for the crew. However, crewmen often resigned or left their ship when in port, and Bureau simply shrugged and went on with his planning.

What happened next is not quite clear, since Bureau and most of his crew were to lose their lives, and different accounts were given of the exact circumstances. The main source is a South American ship's boy names Munos who managed to make his way back to Chile by way of Hawaii, where, in September 1836, he gave an account to the local French consul, Adolphe Barot. Further reports were made when he reached South America and spoke to various merchantmen, including the Americans who had earlier attempted to dissuade Bureau from going to Fiji. Apparently, Bureau had sailed to Fiji, where he left a man named George – or Joseph – to collect trepang from the islanders in exchange for various goods, including muskets, and then went on to Tahiti, where more goods were left to await his return from Fiji. The *Aimable Josephine* was away for almost eight months, Bureau carrying out some local trading, but having to deal with the missionaries who were settling in among the islands, some being English Anglicans or Methodists, others French and Roman Catholics, and few of them sympathetic to Bureau's trading and to what was obviously a quick temper, for some of his crew deserted because they found it impossible to get on with him and seemed not to have been paid any wages.

When Bureau sailed back from Tahiti to eastern Viti Levu, he found that George, whose health was poor and who had begun to believe Bureau was not coming back, had sold most of the trepang to a passing American trader who had taken them to China. Bureau was naturally furious at this dishonesty, but George was apparently forgiven for his misdeeds, when Bureau realised how much pressure the man had been under because of his health and also because of the inter-tribal warfare going on in the region. While more trepang was being collected, Bureau, who had become friendly with some of the local chiefs, agreed to take some groups of warriors from Taveuni to Somosomo and to carry their weapons in exchange for local goods. He believed that helping local chiefs would be useful to his endeavours and even help him eventually to set up a trading post. Instead, it turned him into an enemy to some and an easily manipulated victim to others. Bureau further endangered himself by falling out with a local chief, Missimara, who had stayed on board the *Aimable Josephine*, but was sent ashore when Bureau lost his temper over some bêche-de-mer he had failed to deliver. It is obvious at this point that Bureau had planned for only a short stay in the Fiji archipelago, trading elsewhere while bêche-de-mer were being gathered for him, collecting them and simply sailing off to China. Instead, he found himself wasting time and becoming embroiled in local wars. This led to him becoming an enemy to some of the islanders, which soon spelt his end.

Munos reported how the attack occurred under orders from Missimara: "One of the five natives who were working on board the ship as sailors and a man the captain was quite fond of because he spoke some French, came up to him and warned him that a longboat which belonged to the *Aimable Josephine* and which was anchored not far from the brig was full of water and that it needed urgently to be emptied. The captain got up and using his spyglass looked at the state of the longboat. At that moment, the man hit him brutally with a sharp stick and caused him to fall dead, his head pierced right through. His spyglass fell into the sea. At that same moment, the other natives rushed towards the bow of the vessel and killed the second-in-command and a sailor named Georges. The cook and I rushed into the sailors' quarters and begged for our lives, whereupon the natives told us that we could come back and that they did not intend to kill us. And indeed, once we were back on deck, they did us no harm. Two hours later, Missi Malo, the chief of Viwa, came on board and appeared to be quite saddened by the sight of Captain Bureau lying in a pool of blood, because he was quite fond of him. But Missi Mara, the king of Revu, was more powerful than him. We were sent to the chief's house. During the night, the vessel was emptied of all its shells and other valuable items. Missi Mara then came on board to inspect the ship, and call us, as well as the two sailors who had been ashore when the attack took place and, like us, had sought refuge with Missi Malo, and he threatened to kill us if we did not reveal places where the captain might have hidden some of his possessions. We were forced to climb on board and look for anything we knew about, and soon there was nothing left."

The Fijians tried to dispose of the *Aimable Josephine* and sailed the brig as best they could to Levuka, where they hoped to find some European or American sailors to take her over, but the circumstances under which the vessel had come into their hands meant no one dared to buy it. They took it back to their district as best they could, but it eventually struck a coral reef and lay abandoned for months, gradually disintegrating.

Although the account given by Munos was considered the most reliable, there were other versions circulating in the Pacific, but what was clear was that trading among the islands was becoming increasingly dangerous, and that the intervention of the British and other governments was necessary if merchantmen were to work among the islands and develop a fairly regular trade with China and the Americas. The French government, in particular, was incensed by the murders that had occurred, and although it did not actually send anyone to take revenge, the instructions it had given to the naval commander Jules Dumont d'Urville regarding his voyage of exploration with the ships *Astrolabe* and *Zelee* included references to opening up possibilities for French trade and providing protection to any merchantmen he might meet. The news of the Bureau disaster had reached Paris by the time D'Urville sailed from Toulon in September 1837, and was one of the matters he personally intended to investigate more fully.

He reached the east coast of Viti Levu in mid-October 1838, and after some futile attempt to obtain an apology and some form of reparation for the killing of Bureau and his men, he destroyed the village and a kind of fortress the locals had built, told a friendly chief that he had not come to start a war, but rather to warn the

Home of George Pritchard in Papeete.

locals that a similar punishment awaited "any chief who might try, without cause, to insult a French ship". This done, he sailed away, drafting a full report to the Minister of Marine, which he forwarded to Paris in February 1839 with other details of his exploration of the central Pacific.

Attempts were made to recover some of the goods Bureau was reported to have left in Tahiti and elsewhere, to be given to his children as part of their inheritance, his wife having died a few years earlier. It was found that most of his possessions had been left in the care of an English missionary, George Pritchard, a powerful ally of the young Queen of Tahiti, Pōmare IV to whom he had given most of the items. An alternative version was that Pritchard had merely taken over whatever Bureau had stored and sold them for his own benefit. Pritchard had been working hard to turn Tahiti into a British colony, and to keep out the rival French missionaries. He eventually failed in both endeavours and was forced to leave the island in the early 1840s. However, some compensation for Bureau's goods was obtained and Bureau's young children also received help from the authorities in France.

Emile Bureau's story was told in many ports and long remained as a warning to would-be traders, but it also marked a turning point in the growth of the Pacific Ocean, from an area of bold exploration and daring trading to one of colonisation and mercantile growth. As for the man himself, he is remembered, if at all, as either an unfortunate victim of resentful islanders or as an authoritarian, often ill-tempered ship's captain whose character sealed his own fate in increasingly dangerous times.

8

A Mormon Adventurer

As the years went by and the Pacific world became better known and grew in importance, adventurers tried their hand at winning over the islanders and creating a dominant position over them. Their dream was usually to set up a local independent kingdom, based on the islanders' growing concern over colonisation and their traditional inter-tribal rivalries. Walter Murray Gibson was one of these, a strong personality with a talent for oratory and a gift for persuading people to follow him, whatever his policy or aims seemed to be. He seized opportunities as they presented themselves, and he changed tactics with great ease and apparent honesty. When he was unmasked or the situation caused him to be on the wrong side, he swiftly dealt with the disaster, although he equally swiftly presented the image of an unfortunate victim, calling on people's sympathy and willingness to help.

Gibson was born in March 1822 possibly in England, equally possibly in the United States. He at times stated that he was actually born between the two countries, born at sea on a ship taking his parents from Britain to America. This enabled him to present himself as a national of whichever country best suited his circumstances. He grew up in New York and neighbouring New Jersey, although what he did is not clear. He probably worked as a ship's boy, then as a sailor, going down to South America and to the Caribbean, where it is probable he engaged in gunrunning and vague activities related to the occasional acts of piracy, which still occurred in the region. Gibson had heard a great deal about the wealth that could be made by trading among the Pacific islands, and in the late 1840s or early 1850s, he sailed as the captain of a small brig to Asia and the western Pacific islands.

Walter Murray Gibson, the former Mormon who became a politician.

He apparently traded among the islands of present-day Indonesia, looking for opportunities in the shipping lines dominated by the Dutch and considering the possibility of working with the locals as an adviser and to some extent a local ruler, a formula he was to adopt for years to come. There had been several uprisings in Java and Sumatra against the Dutch East India Company, the Vereenigde Oostindische Compagnie or V.O.C., whose trade and exploration went back to the early 17th century, but the Company's troops had defeated the locals on every occasion. Gibson offered his help to a group of rebels in Sumatra in 1852 and seemed successful for a while, but he was caught and sent to Batavia (present-day Jakarta), where he was sentenced to 15 years' imprisonment for treason and anti-Dutch activities. He spent 16 months in jail, then managed to escape and make his way back to North America.

Now penniless, Gibson was determined to rebuild what he saw as a promising future in the growing world of the Pacific. He wrote an account of his misfortunes at the hands of the Dutch, entitled *The Prison of Weltevreden: and a Glance at the East Indian Archipelago*, which was published in 1855 and which he took around to several states, giving talks on his adventures and the Pacific, which his audiences greatly appreciated, as much on account of his convincing eloquence as of the image of the strange and entrancing world he impressively described. He travelled to Utah, the state of the Church of Jesus Christ of Latter-day Saints, known as the Mormons. There, he converted to Mormonism and approached the church's leader, Brigham Young, with the suggestion that he be sent to the Pacific, to the Hawaiian islands in particular, and there establish a Mormon church among the locals. Several Mormons had already travelled to the Pacific, preaching the new faith and establishing several posts. Brigham Young gave him his approval as well as some funds, and in 1861 Walter Gibson sailed to Hawaii as a missionary.

He was successful – his personality and skills as a public speaker soon gathering followers. He stated his intention to build up a Mormon colony among the islanders and bought land on the island of Lanai. This would enable him to develop farming and trade, as well as giving the Mormons a strong foothold, Lanai being fairly centrally situated among the Hawaiian islands. The problem was that, although he used money provided by the Mormon Church, he bought the estate in his own name. He also offered positions to several islanders in what he promised would be a major Mormon colony, but did so in exchange for cash and sundry island products he then sold on to passing merchantmen. If his local listeners found some of the Church of Latter-day Saints' religious tenets difficult to accept or integrate with their own traditions, Gibson simply adapted them with convincing eloquence to fit their preferences, all the while developing his own ability to speak their Polynesian dialect.

Rumours of Gibson's dominance in Lanai and of his tendency to alter Mormon beliefs to suit his circumstances led to an investigation by other Mormons. He was accused of preaching false doctrines, administering the colony for his own gain and, when it was discovered that he had used Mormon funds to buy land for himself, embezzlement of church funds. He was excommunicated, but by now he felt strong enough to retaliate by expelling anyone who did not support him. This included the physical expulsion of his opponents, thereby strengthening his own position. He was now able to revert to his earlier practice of using for his own advantage any islanders' dissatisfaction with the growing presence of Europeans, and turned to local politics, putting himself forward as a servant of the islanders.

Having lost the earlier foothold provided by his links with the Mormons, he rebuilt his reputation by publishing a newspaper, which he called the *Nuhou*, commenting on the political situation, the need of the Hawaiians for sound administration, and his own talents, which he offered to the people. *Nuhou* was significantly made up of two words: the English word "new" and its equivalent in the local tongue, *hou*. Its subtitle clearly indicated his aim: "Devoted to the material needs of the Hawaiian archipelago". It was first published in 1873 and gradually led him into the political arena as a supporter of King Kalākaua. He successfully ran for the Hawaiian House of Representatives in 1878 as a member of the King's Party and promoted himself as "the voice of Hawaiians" – a

King Kalākaua

claim that cemented his opposition to the growing American influence in the islands and also reflects his earlier claim as a defender of the people of Sumatra against the Dutch administrators. To strengthen his position he took over another publication, the *Pacific Commercial Advertiser* (later renamed the *Honolulu Advertiser*), although once again his purchase of the newspaper led to claims that he had not paid the due amount and cheated the sellers. Nevertheless, both publications were craftily used by Gibson to advance his own views and to mock his opponents. Unfailingly, however, he supported the king and his party.

His efforts were rewarded by King Kalākaua who appointed him Minister of Foreign Affairs in 1882, a post he held for four years and that positioned him as a straight opponent of the United States. In 1886, he was for a brief time Minister of the Interior and Prime Minister, returning to Foreign Affairs in October 1886, a position he held until July 1887.

His influence over King Kalākaua was evident, but it did not last. Kalākaua became concerned at Gibson's plans and his rash moves, which only served to increase a sense of animosity among the Americans who had settled in the islands, including those who regarded themselves as Mormons but whom Gibson now viewed as his enemies. They blamed him for manipulating the king into drawing up and signing the Constitution of the Kingdom of Hawaii, and became even more concerned when he proposed to build a Pacific Empire centred on the Hawaiian kingdom, which would gradually extend to include a number of island groups. There were also murmurs about his own enrichment, whispers of embezzlement and shady deals. In July 1887, the king required him and others in the cabinet to resign, whereupon his enemies began to talk of investigations into Gibson's affairs and an eventual trial. The threats were serious, there were attacks made on him by armed groups, and Gibson was forced to flee to San Francisco, where he died, again penniless and friendless, in January 1888.

The islands, which were going through a period of economic hardship, were taken over for a while by a so-called Committee of Safety promoted by the American consul. They then became the Republic of Hawaii in 1894, and, after more instability, this was in 1898 finally proclaimed a United States territory. These troubled times did no harm to the memory of Walter Gibson who was still regarded by some as a Hawaiian personality of note. His body was returned to the islands and buried in Honolulu in the presence of numerous grieving Hawaiians. He might have failed in his endeavours, but his personality and his skill in emotionally manipulating people had earned him a posthumous reward.

9

Shipwrecked Victims

The Pacific being the world's largest ocean, so little known to navigators in earlier times, with inadequate maps, uncharted reefs and incorrect locations for so many island groups, the number of shipwrecks that occurred over the years is tragically high. Ships simply disappeared and, in the absence of the modern facilities we now take for granted, such as wireless and electronic messaging, their fate remained unknown – until they reappeared in their home ports or elsewhere. Nor could they ask for help from their home ports if some misfortune befell them. When disaster struck, it was in a frightening void, and the survivors could only struggle as best they could, making their way in desperation towards an uncertain target, often in the roughest of seas, through the remains of a cyclone that had destroyed their ship in the first place.

Sometimes, a dispute on board ship led to sailors deserting or being abandoned on some island, to survive, await the arrival of another vessel or find a way to move on. One sad case was that of a ship's boy, Narcisse Pelletier, who was left behind in 1858 by survivors of the shipwrecked *Saint-Paul*, alone on a small island off Cape Flattery in northern Queensland. He was only 14 years old, but struggled first on his own, then as part of an Aboriginal settlement for another 17 years. He was eventually rescued by a British pearling vessel, the *John Bell*, and in time made his way back to France where he was hailed as a hero and ended his life as a respected lighthouse keeper.

The number of shipwrecks that occurred in the Pacific over the years is considerable – in fact, the real total is unknown – and it has produced a number of stories about the survivors, many of whom survived because they managed to be accepted by the local people. Before Narcisse Pelletier, for instance, we have the case of James Murrell, a sailor on board

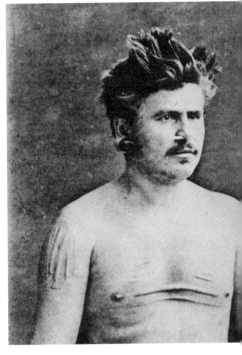

Narcisse Pelletier, shipwrecked as a boy, as he appeared after 17 years living with the Aboriginals.

the *Peruvian*, a vessel of some 300 tons, which had sailed from Sydney in February 1846, planning to take a shipment of timber and other material to China. The ship was owned mostly by its captain, a Scotsman named Pitkethly, who was accompanied by his wife and his brother and, as passengers, the Wilmot family, with two children and a nurse, and J.P. Quarry and his young daughter. The crew consisted of some 15 sailors. The weather was fine as they left Sydney Harbour, but the ship simply vanished and its fate was not known for another 17 years – when James Murrell was rescued by a small group of settlers who were making their way along the northern Queensland coast, and was able to tell his story.

Within a few days of leaving Sydney, the *Peruvian* had been assailed by a tornado that had torn its sails and been left to drift helplessly along the coast until it struck a reef. The officer on duty was thrown out by the suddenness of the shock and drowned in the swirling waves. Pitkethly's brother, who was acting as second-in-command, tried to launch the ship's boat, but he too was drowned and the longboat was dashed to pieces by the reef. All that could be done was to hurriedly construct a makeshift raft with pieces of the masts and some loose planks. A few supplies were lashed onto it – nine tins of dried meat, some drinking water and one precious bottle of brandy. There was room on it for Pitkethly and his wife, the Wilmot and Quarry families and the rest of the crew. But there was no means of steering the clumsy craft, which drifted roughly north, with the men trying as best they could to keep away from the reef and make for the coast, which they knew was not too far to their west.

A couple of weeks went by, with the food and drinking water running out. Attempts to catch some fish, to be eaten raw, were made, and a few unwise seagulls landing on the raft were also caught and eaten raw. A shower or two of rain provided the only drinking water, but there was no way to catch what fell, because of the absence of any pots: the meat cans, once emptied, had been thrown overboard. In the third week, Quarry died and was buried at sea with minimal ceremony. Then one of the children died of hunger and soon the Wilmot couple followed. Time went by and at least one body was thrown overboard each day, except for one which was used by Captain Pitkethly as bait for a shark that had been following the raft, which was killed and hauled aboard, to be used as food – and partly as drink for those desperate enough to suck its insides.

Finally, land appeared and after having drifted for 42 days, the survivors, seven in all, were able to set foot on land. They had no idea where they were, and all they could see around them was desert and dried bush. They were in fact a short distance from Cape Cleveland, near what is now the city of Townsville, but which in those days was still uninhabited. They found a few oysters on the rocks, which kept them going for a few days, led by the example of Mrs Pitkethly who showed herself to be a firm leader in spite of what most of them believed to be a hopeless situation. One of the men died a couple of days after landing, and another who had discovered what seemed to be an Aboriginal's canoe along a creek was drowned while trying to bring it along to the shoreline. The remainder, having roughly estimated their position, continued to plod their way north, hoping to find a settlement, but they were being followed by a group of locals who came out towards them, fascinated and a little afraid of the strange white humans who looked to them more like spirits from another world than real people.

One group took away Captain Pitkethly and his wife; another took away Murrell, his companion and the young Wilmot boy, both of whom died within a few weeks. The Aboriginals were attentive to the Pitkethlys, gave them food and shelter and effectively adopted them, but Pitkethly was in poor health and died after an estimated six months; his wife soon gave up after this, worn out by the hardships which life with a nomadic group involved, so that the only survivor was Murrell who was aged 23 and who was still strong enough to hunt with the tribe, learn their practices and in time their language. The years went by, and he lived happily enough among the people who had seemingly adopted him without any second thoughts. At times, they saw ships sailing not far from the shore, but James Murrell was unable to wave to them for help, partly because this would cause the Aboriginals to consider him a traitor, as it was evident by then that the Europeans were their enemies, shooting at any who ventured too close, and partly because he himself looked like one of the tribe, practically nude, with a tough sunburned skin and straggly untidy hair.

But the colonisation of northern Queensland was proceeding, however slowly. Murrell was told by his co-tribesmen that some Europeans mounted on strange animals – for they had never seen horses before – were proceeding north a few miles inland, driving small herds of cattle and sheep. But it was unwise to go too near them, as they tended to fire their murderous rifles at anyone who came too close. But one day he cautiously crept towards a hut which a couple of whites had built, part of a sheep station that was being established in the district. He called out a "hello", which he hoped would be understood as English, but the man who came out saw what he thought was an Aboriginal and called out to his mate to bring out his rifle. Struggling with a language he had not used for years, Murrell shouted out "No kill me. I British man shipwrecked on this land". It was enough to be told to come into the hut, arms held high, and begin to narrate his tragic adventures and his life among the small group. He learned that the date was now 25 January 1863, and that he had spent 17 years among the tribe. He had had no way of calculating the passing of time, a matter of no consequence to the Aboriginals. The two settlers had now accepted him and offered him tea and bread, the taste of which he found strange after so many years. They laughed and promised he would have more surprises as he returned to European life. But first, he insisted on going back to the tribe and saying his farewells. This gave him the opportunity of explaining to them that, while the Europeans were settling on what could be called their lands, they did not intend to take away from them their hunting and fishing places, and warning them at the same time that the Europeans were too numerous and too well-armed for the tribe to try to fight them. He would later use his knowledge of Aboriginal life to plead their case with the administrators and settlers he would meet. He was farewelled with a mixture of solemnity and sorrow by the people he had lived with for so long; then he returned to the hut to wash himself with soap and to put on some clothes the two men lent him.

He travelled to the growing settlement of Port Denison, present-day Bowen, where he told his story and was made welcome by the population. He went on to Rockhampton, where he was introduced to the local administrator and offered several positions, one as interpreter in a survey of the coastline up to Cairns, the other as storekeeper in Bowen. He married and had one child, but died in late October 1865, aged 41. He is buried in Bowen and a small memorial has been erected to commemorate his adventures.

Being shipwrecked somewhere along the Australian shore or along a route that was used by a number of trading vessels was, even in those early days, often safer than being lost on some Pacific island. All too often, the wreck occurred in uncharted waters, the navigators being uncertain of their location and consequently unsure of which direction they should take if they were fortunate enough to have a workable ship's boat or to construct some form of raft to which they could attach a few sails. Surviving on the island, doing a little fishing and hunting for food inland, in the hope that some passing vessel might be able to rescue them, was another possibility, but in all these cases they had to cope with the presence of islanders who viewed them as potential enemies, invaders and threats to their own settlements. This explains why a number of shipwrecks remain a mystery, apart from tales sometimes told by Pacific islanders of strange and evil spirits whom their ancestors had beaten back or destroyed to protect their tribe.

The tale of the trading vessel *Plato* is easier to reconstruct because one man survived from its shipwreck and was able to outline what had happened to his ship in May 1873. This was John Collins, sometimes also referred to as Jeremiah Collins, one of the ship's seven sailors. They had sailed from Newcastle, in New South Wales, with a shipment of coal and other supplies for China, under the command of Captain Thomas Hart, his second Thomas Glasgow, his boatswain Thomas Pickering, five sailors, a Chinese cook and a ship's boy – a total complement of ten men, sufficient for a three-master like the *Plato*. They had sailed north for ten days, keeping clear of the Great Barrier Reef and intending to make their way across the Coral Sea into the southern Pacific. The area was still ill-charted – Arrowsmith's famous map of the Pacific Ocean of 1851 struggled with the cluster of reefs and islands west of the Solomons – but it was a customary route for vessels going from eastern Australia to Asia, so Thomas Hart felt, after a day of scrutinising the horizon and marking his charts, that he could take a rest and leave the course to Thomas Glasgow. Unfortunately, after a little more than an hour he was roughly awakened. The *Plato* had struck a reef a short distance from Huon Island and the shouts of the men made it clear that the ship was stuck fast and beginning to take in water. The situation was rapidly worsening with the *Plato* beginning to list, so he ordered the whaleboat to be lowered, filled with as much food and drinking water as it could hold, and rowed towards the small uninhabited island.

They spent 11 days on Huon, but with no likelihood of another vessel sailing past and rescuing them, they decided their only course was to make for Timor to the north-west or, if the winds and the currents were favourable, to try to reach some part of northern Australia. They constructed a rough shelter on the whaleboat, although they had almost no spare sails or rags to use for sleeping or resting. And Hart soon realised that what remained of the drinking water was insufficient for a long journey. He decided to try to reach Port Adam, the southernmost point of San Cristobal, one of the Solomon Islands. Struggling on, they reached a small island situated off Santa Ana, one of the easternmost of the Solomon Islands. They put into a narrow inlet, hoping to find a stream of fresh water and some fruit, but soon found themselves surrounded by several canoes which had emerged from some nearby village. The islanders seemed friendly enough and half a dozen men agreed to go ashore in the canoes and were actually offered food, but when they returned, intending to get back into their boat, they saw that the Melanesians' canoes had all been hauled ashore, and as they turned to argue with the islanders, they were attacked, all six being killed. Captain Hart immediately ordered their boat to make for the open sea, but the four survivors found themselves surrounded by shouting islanders who attacked them with arrows and lumps of sharp coral. According to Collins, there were about 50 Melanesians, all shouting and shooting arrows. Hart managed to steer the craft a short distance away, but Thomas Glasgow was struck by an arrow – Collins dramatically insisted that it had gone straight to his heart – and he fell overboard where his assailants finished him off. Hart was next, and a sailor, Peter Stripe, fearing that he would be captured and tortured, killed himself.

John Collins had been hit by several arrows, but they had struck only his legs and the wounds were not severe. He jumped into the sea, hoping to swim ashore and escape into the bush, but he was caught within a few minutes and dragged ashore. He fully expected to be finished off in the same way as he had seen his companions, but he was taken to the nearby village, where a couple of arrows that were still stuck to his legs were carefully removed and his wounds tended with water and leaves which he assumed had therapeutic value. He was fed and kept in a hut under the watchful eye of a large Melanesian, to make sure he would not escape. He was cared for in this way for over three months, and in time learned that, according to the islanders' beliefs, if their gods had not intended that he should be seriously wounded, it was their duty to care for him and adopt him as one of theirs. He would later report how he had felt to be thus regarded and prepared himself to become one of the tribe – at least for as long as fate did not come to his rescue.

The islanders to some extent must have been proud to have among them a white man who seemed to have been given to them by their tribal gods, for they did not hide the fact of his presence from the neighbouring tribes. Little by little, the news passed along the islands, until some missionaries in Valua, in the New Hebrides, found out that a white man, a sailor who was the sole survivor of a shipwreck, was living in the Solomon Islands. They mentioned this to Captain Suckling, commander of the British Royal Navy ship, HMS *Fox*, who was stationed in the New Hebrides. Suckling decided at once that the man should be rescued, especially as he was believed to be a British sailor, and he set sail for the island of San Cristobal, where he hoped to find another British ship but if not to sail on alone towards Santa Ana. He met an American brig, the *Hallie Jackson*, whose captain promptly offered to help him, and they sailed on towards Mary Island. The American, Fuller, was slightly ahead when he sighted a man waving on the beach. He ordered a boat to be lowered and make for the shore, but by the time it arrived the islanders had dragged the man away into one of their canoes. Captain Suckling also came alongside, and the two ships blocked the small bay and their longboats, well armed, made for the shore. However, the shoreline was full of mangroves, preventing them from actually reaching land. There was a tense confrontation between the islanders and the sailors, but the rescuers realised that fighting for Collins would probably cause the islanders to kill him. He was brought out, under guard, to address the men of the *Fox* and the *Hallie Jackson*, and explain who he was and the situation in which he found himself. Then bargaining started, and it was finally agreed that the islanders would release him in exchange for three axes, two large knives, a musket and some sea pearls. The barter concluded, John Collins was handed over to the men of the *Fox*, and the ships returned to San Cristobal, providing Collins with an opportunity to detail his adventures. He had survived among the natives for four months, and would boast – or accept the sailors' teasing – that he was worth three axes and a total of five knives, which he insisted were of the best quality.

Captain Suckling reported to the commander of another British naval vessel, the HMS *Dido,* which had recently arrived at San Cristobal, and the two men decided to go to Port Adam, where the men of the *Plato* had been attacked, both to check that there were actually no survivors, and also to carry out reprisals against the locals. Their excuse was that there was a need to impress the islanders that Europeans were now navigating along the islands and in fact establishing themselves in the Solomons, and that attacks like the one against the *Plato* would not be tolerated. They did find three islanders who had apparently been part of the incident and took them away as prisoners to Malaita; what eventually happened to them is not recorded. In his report, the captain of the *Dido* does not mention any reprisals against the villages of Mary Island, so it can be assumed that he felt that enough had been done. He returned with John Collins and released him to make his way back to Australia, where he could find work and hold audiences in thrall by narrating his misadventures. At this point, he disappears from history.

His tale is but one of many told of shipwrecks, murders and enslavement, which occurred during the second half of the 19th century. In many cases, the victims were the unlucky consequence of the brutality and ill-treatment carried out by Europeans: blackbirders kidnapping and starving islanders, traders sailing past and stealing food, firing at the islanders, and inflicting pointless damage to their canoes and villages. It took time for the Pacific world to settle down and earn the name Ferdinand Magellan had bestowed on it in 1521, "Mar Pacifico", but unhappily the 20th century would see warfare and brutality return to its waters.

10

Colonial Scoundrels

*T*he exploration of the Pacific, the last great region of the world to be revealed to European and Asian nations, was marked by often brutal incidents, providing opportunities for unscrupulous or untrustworthy characters. Dominating the early scene were rivalries between Spanish, Dutch and American traders and settlers, as well as fear and distrust on the part of the islanders who were themselves the descendants of early explorers who, centuries earlier, had ventured into unknown seas and settled in uninhabited territories.

Gradually, the Europeans took over and developed most of the Pacific, some escaping from their world of grime and poverty, others sent unwillingly to convicts settlements – to Australia for the British and to New Caledonia for the French. Most of them were later freed, the majority choosing to return home, but a number of them took their chance to settle, as liberated convicts, into their new home.

They did not always reveal to those they met that they had been brought down into the Pacific against their will. For instance, the famous character who called himself Captain Jackson Barry had, it seems, been brought out to Australia as a young teenager, some time in 1829 or 1830, possibly as a punishment for some minor theft, and handed over as a servant to a local butcher. He was freed – or escaped – and found different occupations, possibly as a bushranger for a while, then as a sailor, including on a whaling ship. He later told stories of how he had been shipwrecked, surviving on one occasion by clinging to the floating carcass of a dead whale.

Barry found his way to the Californian goldfields, which in the early 1850s promised great riches to those who ventured there, but soon returned to Sydney, setting up shop as a butcher in Ballarat near Melbourne, and calling himself Jimmy Ducks. Then came news of the Otago goldrush in New Zealand, which attracted numerous prospectors. But Barry knew that prospecting for gold was a hard, backbreaking job, and that finding gold was largely a matter of luck. He wisely thought that supplying the immigrants with food and other supplies was likely to be more profitable, and he crossed to New Zealand and opened a butcher's shop in a growing settlement called The Junction, later renamed Cromwell.

Hundreds of hopeful prospectors had settled in the district, with only one thought in mind: to find a goldmine. This had led to their being exploited by the few traders who roamed the district, including a meat dealer monopoly that Barry had soon identified and decided to break. He gave his premises the grand title of Victoria and Sydney Butchery, and proudly displayed his motto "Free Trade and No Monopoly". Within weeks, he had beaten the other supplier and brought down the price of meat, roughly cut into large chunks, to a mere sixpence a pound. Hailed by the residents and the settlers of the district, he expanded into a general dealer in livestock and farming supplies, as well as an auctioneer, a job for which, with his personality and his talent for impressive tales, he was particularly suited. When Cromwell began to feel it needed a mayor, he was elected to the sound of cheers and clinking glasses.

The so-called election had lasted all day and well into the night, with the electors making their way home by 4 a.m. Cromwell, however, was not fully incorporated as a town, and when it was, a few months later, a new formal election had to be held. Barry was re-elected with no difficulty – except that he forgot to hold the required swearing-in ceremony. So a new election was held, a mere formality, but one which enabled Barry to boast in his later years that he had been elected mayor three times in a 12-month period. A mayor, however, was expected to act as a chairman, not as a loud, bossy character, which he was, and when he happened to be away from Cromwell, a vote of censure was passed. When he returned, he asked who had put the motion and knocked down the councillor who admitted that he had. He then crossed out the motion from the records and dared anyone else to challenge him. All this was expressed in the colourful language for which Barry had become famous, and which brought about another public argument, this time with the local teacher who complained that the mayor was setting a bad example to the children of Cromwell.

His butchery business seemed to prosper, but it turned out that Barry was simply not paying his bills, and the local bank manager forced him to sell his shop to at least partly pay off his overdraft. Barry, using his talents as an orator and a storyteller to turn the locals' attention back to gold mining, founded a prospecting company under the impressive name of "The Royal Standard Syndicate". The miners he sent out to what seemed a promised land did find a small quantity of gold, which Barry displayed around the town. He then offered his shares for sale, telling his listeners he wanted everyone to enjoy the wealth that lay hidden in the hills, and with the proceeds he was able to pay off most of his outstanding debts. At which point, he left Cromwell. The Royal Standard Syndicate disappeared not long after.

Barry opened a pub in nearby Queenstown, and in his usual style gave it a grandiose name, the Prince of Wales Hotel. He also tried his luck as an auctioneer, describing whatever he was selling in florid terms, and in fact drawing audiences who were more interested in his stories than in the goods he was trying to sell. He realised that there might be more money to be made out of storytelling than in commerce, and at the end of 1870 he gave a lecture on his adventures around the Pacific and in New Zealand, which drew a large crowd and led him to travel to Sydney and attract similar audiences to meetings that fascinated his listeners sufficiently for them to pay a fee to attend and, in some cases, for personal advice on their own chances of finding wealth in the goldfields or in the South Seas.

He travelled back to New Zealand, giving more talks, including some about his adventures in Australia, and made his way to Wellington, where he tried to persuade the government to send him to England as the country's publicity agent. He failed, but he made his own way to Britain and started giving his usual colourful talks to working men and others who were thinking of emigrating to New Zealand. He also wrote a book, *Up and Down, or Fifty Years Colonial Experiences*, which was fairly successful, although Thomas Bracken, the author of New Zealand's national anthem, who helped him to write it, cut out most of the colourful terms for which Barry was renowned. After a while, he returned to New Zealand and, by now calling himself Captain Barry, started giving a new series of talks, under the broad title of "Kings and Chiefs

I have Met and Cannibals I have Seen". In days before films or television existed, he found it easy to attract audiences, especially when in Nelson he bought the carcass of a 75-foot whale, which he displayed as an illustration of what he claimed to have used to survive a shipwreck. He later sold it to the Otago Museum – he planned to travel to Australia and it was far too cumbersome to take with him.

He spent several years in Australia, travelling and giving his by now famous lectures, announcing that this was to be his final tour of an Australian township, a claim which helped his advertising campaigns, even though he was willing to come back or stay a little longer if the audiences warranted it. He seldom paid for his accommodation, finding it fairly easy to persuade landlords that his presence drew large enough crowds to their bars to make his stay profitable for them. He published a rehash of his book, with the title *Past and Present, and Men of the Times*, which he sold to his listeners, something he would do again some years later under a new title, *Adventures and Experiences of a Pioneer Colonist*.

Back in New Zealand, he gave more talks. He was now in his seventies and beginning to tire a little, but never ceased to build his reputation. He asked the government to send him as its representative at Queen Victoria's Golden Jubilee celebration in London, but was turned down. He then asked for a state pension, but was told to wait for the old age pension scheme that Prime Minister Richard Seddon was about to introduce. He then declared that he would stand for a parliamentary seat in Auckland, but this failed to eventuate. He died in Christchurch in his eighties, a patient at Sunnyside Hospital which cared for the frail and mentally unstable elderly. He was still claiming that he had been a hero of the Pacific, a promoter of gold mining and the founding mayor of Cromwell.

Barry was but one of the many strange figures who appeared in Australia and New Zealand during the goldrushes – or who called themselves "Captain". George Fairweather Moonlight was an early settler who called himself Captain Moonlight and was sometimes referred to as Captain America. He was born in Scotland in 1832 and had worked as a young boy on the herring boats that sailed into the stormy North Sea. After some six years, he had signed on as a seaman on a trading vessel, still little more than a youth, but toughened by hard toil. He had never attended a school, but had acquired a few skills which earned him some respect among his fellow sailors. However, it was not long before he deserted: his ship had put into American ports, he had heard about the Californian goldrush, and he decided to try his luck among the masses of tough prospectors searching for wealth in the wilderness of western America. He does not appear to have been very successful, and we find him in Australia in the late 1850s, apparently working with some relatives he had come across, but the Otago goldrush attracted him, as it did so many others, and in 1861 he started work in the Nelson and Buller areas.

He was much admired for his boldness and his willingness to set off alone in back-country areas, seeking gold. Tales grew around him: that he was a foundling discovered abandoned on a fisherman's doorstep and called "moonlight" because the moon illuminated the waif; that he tended to vanish, doing a moonlight flit, whenever he came upon a gold nugget; or more simply that he preferred to travel at night, alone and rather ghostlike. However, by 1865, he had settled down, married and eventually gave up searching for gold. Instead, he opened an accommodation house in the Maruia Valley and some time later bought the Commercial Hotel in the township of Murchison. He was successful for a while, but floods ruined the area, his wife died, and he found himself ruined and chased by angry creditors. There was only one way he could repay them – or as some claimed – avoid them, and that was to go back to fossicking for gold. He was only partly rewarded by a few discoveries, but then totally disappeared. People suspected he had fled the district, but after a couple of months his body was found in the bush: he had died alone in the bleak world of inland Westland, aged 52.

He has at times been confused with another Captain Moonlight, Andrew George Scott, an Australia bushranger who had come from Ireland – which was one of the reasons why Fairweather, who was a Scotsman, was often confused with him. His father was a clergyman, who had emigrated to New Zealand in 1861 with his family and settled in the Coromandel district. Andrew, by then

The house of George Fairweather, known as Captain Moonlight, in Maruia, Nelson.

aged 19, worked for a while as a teacher and a member of the local militia. However, although he was a gifted young man, there was a darker side to his character and while some were ready to provide him with good references, others whispered that he could not be trusted. Refused a position in the armed constabulary, he moved to Australia in early 1868, worked for a while for the Anglican Church in Melbourne and Ballarat, but robbed a bank and fled with the proceeds. He went to Sydney, living for a while off the money he had stolen, then started issuing worthless cheques and bought a small yacht, appropriately named the *Why-Not*, and tried to sail to Fiji.

He was caught and given a 12-month sentence, part of which he served in a lunatic asylum because he had feigned madness to excuse his actions. Then, the investigators of the Ballarat robbery caught up with him, and he was sentenced to ten years' hard labour. He had defended himself in court, speaking and joking for hours and entertaining the crowd, which made him famous among the locals but this did not weaken the judge who added an extra year to his sentence. Imprisoned in Pentridge goal in Victoria, famous for being the final resting place of the bushranger Ned Kelly, he was a troublesome and often violent inmate. His guards were glad to see him released early, in 1879, but less enthused by the series of public meetings he began to hold, calling for prison reform and a restructuring of the penal service.

He was soon to become famous for a less savoury incident: a raid on a sheep station near Wagga Wagga, where the gang he led took several hostages, including the two young children of the local hotelkeeper, and fought a battle with the pursuing police group. The result was three deaths, leading to a new trial for Moonlight, this time for murder. He was hanged on 20 January 1880. He might have been the son of a parson and a lay reader, but under the name which he had adopted of Captain Moonlight (sometimes spelt Moonlite), he had become one of Australia's more famous rogues.

Rogues, cranks and traffickers continued to try their luck in Australia and New Zealand during the 19th century, helped by the slow and often inadequate means of communications between the two countries and between the various townships. Some disappeared by simply changing countries, as is sometimes said of James Mackenzie, a Scotsman who had made his way to Australia in his twenties, but moved to Nelson, in New Zealand, in the early 1850s, by which time he was in his thirties. He later claimed to have made good money in the cattle trade, and was looking for opportunities in New Zealand, but he was little known and no one took much notice of him until, in March 1855, farm hands looking for missing sheep in the back country of South Canterbury sighted him with a large flock of sheep and a dog which became famous as Friday, a most faithful animal.

He was arrested as a sheep stealer, but replied that he was merely a drover for their owner. Then he escaped through the little known region, which is referred to as the Mackenzie Country. He reappeared a hundred miles away in the port of Lyttelton, which suggests he was trying to make his way back to Australia. He was charged with sheep stealing, but either refused to reply to questions, or answered in Gaelic. He claimed that he was, like his fellow Scotsmen back home, a victim of British oppression, and refused to recognise the judge. To make things worse, he twice escaped from the jail where he was being held. He was sentenced to five years' hard labour, but another judge later reviewed the case, and he was pardoned in January 1856. At which point, he disappeared, probably back to Australia, but leaving enough speculation and legends to become a famous figure in local folklore.

Not all early scoundrels were outright thieves. Some, like Arthur Worthington, appeared on the scene as orators and philosophers. His real name is believed to have been Samuel Oakley Crawford, born in the United States in 1847, and he is said to have begun life as an itinerant Methodist preacher. He had a tendency to marry rich widows, and then leave them when the money ran out. He was first jailed for obtaining money by false pretences in 1870. This did not stop him from marrying again, and he is believed to have married five women in the States before fleeing to New Zealand in 1890 and changing his name to Arthur Bently Worthington.

He charmed audiences with his sermons, no longer as a Methodist, but as "an apostle of truth and reason". He collected money from his followers, both for himself and for an eventual "Temple of Truth". But true Methodists, led by the prominent minister John Hosking of Christchurch, had begun to investigate his past, and discovered his numerous bigamous marriages. When he forsook the wife he had brought with him from America, and arranged a marriage with yet another woman in August 1895, most of his followers deserted him and police enquiries began. He fled to Tasmania, where he was unsuccessful in his endeavours, and returned to Christchurch in September 1897. He tried to give more lectures, but was too discredited to obtain new followers, and his appearance at the Oddfellows Hall resulted in a riot involving almost 6,000 people. He left for Sydney, but after more frauds he was arrested and sentenced to seven years' imprisonment. Back in the United States, he engaged in new fraudulent activities, usually helping himself to church funds, and was once more arrested, dying in prison in 1917.

Not all the shady characters who toured Australia and New

Zealand in those days were men. One who became famous as a light-fingered traveller was Amy Bock, born in Australia in May 1859, who started work as a teacher in Tasmania and might have had a successful career or found a good husband had it not been for her tendency to steal goods from shops she visited. Her claim that she was merely buying goods on credit and intended to pay for them later were ignored and she was summoned to court, whereupon she fled to Auckland where her father now lived. She obtained a job as a governess and was popular with the children, although less with her employers as she tended to help

Amy Bock, famous kleptomaniac and con-artist, who married a wealthy woman while disguised as Percival Leonard Redwood.

herself to their money. Arrested and charged, she pleaded guilty, wept, talked about her deceased mother and her loneliness. She was let off with a caution, found another job but was again arrested for petty thieving. Her acting talents were considerable. Indeed, at one stage she had thought of trying the stage, but actresses had a bad reputation at the time and were sometimes written off as little more than prostitutes. Being a governess, a cook or, a much preferred job, a carer for an elderly lady, was much better. Shopping for them enabled her to write things up on her employer's tab or simply slip the odd item into her bag.

When caught, she excused herself by claiming she had forgotten her purse or was simply absent-minded or worried about her employer's state of health. However, she was arrested in May 1886, having fled from Christchurch to Wellington with unpaid goods, and this time she was sentenced to a month's hard labour. She was again arrested for theft and was sentenced to six months in Caversham Industrial School, a prison-like institution in Dunedin, where she volunteered as a teacher for the other inmates. Then she showed the superintendent a letter from an elderly sick aunt who was pleading for her help; her request for early release, however, was turned down when the superintendent discovered the aunt did not actually exist. After her release, several minor thefts got her two more stays in prison, but she moved to Dunedin where she was less known, and obtained a job as housekeeper. When her employer was away, Amy Bock pawned her furniture and took the proceeds before leaving the district. She was soon caught and received a three-year sentence. Upon her release, she moved to Timaru, but she stole her employer's watch, and she was sent back to prison.

She decided not just to change towns, but to get a new name. Calling herself Mary Shannon, she travelled to Wellington and Auckland, and fooled investors into giving her money for a large poultry farm she was planning to build. The fraud was exposed and after serving another two years, she moved to Rakaia, calling herself Amy Chanel. She found that writing cheques was a good way to obtain money from gullible traders, and continued to use different names, at least eight different ones, but once more was caught and sentenced to three years.

Her next trick was to change her sex, and reappear as Percival Leonard Redwood, claiming on a couple of occasions that she was the nephew of the popular Archbishop of Wellington, Francis Redwood. Pretending to be a man of substance, she travelled around Otago, and eventually courted a wealthy woman, Agnes Ottaway. Money was easily advanced for the forthcoming wedding, which actually took place in April 1909. Amy Bock was no doubt intending to vanish after the ceremony, but her landlady, annoyed by Percival's lengthy unpaid bill, had gone through her belongings, discovered the truth and informed the police. Bock was arrested, declared to be a habitual criminal and sentenced to a period of indeterminate imprisonment. However, she always behaved well in prison, offering to help as a cook and a teacher, and she was paroled in less than three years.

At that point, she moved to the country and started to give acting and piano performances. She even married, although this time the groom was an elderly farmer. She led an exemplary life for a while, but she still ran up debts, and even raised funds to buy a piano for the local hall, although she kept for herself the money she raised. Arrested, but merely fined, Bock travelled to Hamilton, still pilfering, and was yet again arrested for various charges of fraud. She was then an elderly but dignified lady of some 72 years, and the magistrates decided she could not be sent back to a bleak prison cell. Instead, she was given two years' probation and ordered to live in a Salvation Army home. She died there in August 1943, the most famous kleptomaniac in New Zealand or Australia.

11

Chinese Victims

For many centuries, the Pacific Ocean had been to the Chinese a world of mystery and danger. They fished along its shores, making a good living, as they did along the banks of the rivers that flowed down into its waters. They traded with each other, cautiously sailing in bamboo craft along the shore, but never out of sight of land, for the few unlucky ones whom unexpected storms or currents dragged out into the vast ocean never returned. The old wise men spoke of many mysterious islands, of monsters and at times of wondrous discoveries. And indeed, there were navigators like the famous Hsu Fu who ventured out and did return, but they were few, until other sailors emerged from other parts of Asia, from Malaysia and India; and in time white people too appeared and brought both riches and danger.

Once the great ocean had opened out, the Chinese found new opportunities for trade and for adventures, like fossicking for gold in distant lands or labouring in faraway islands, but always striving to return and be buried in the sacred homeland of their ancestors. Some, however, fell victim to exploiters, men called blackbirders, who tricked them into the equivalent of slavery on distant plantations or mines, tempting them on board a ship and sailing away without their consent or often even their knowledge until the vessel had moved away from the shore, effectively kidnapping them and eventually selling them into the equivalent of slavery.

They were often victims of other Chinese who worked for the blackbirders and recruited them by promising that they would be taken to goldmines to fossick for themselves and brought back in due course, happy to reward those who had recruited them and, so they claimed, had contributed to the cost of their voyage. There were a number of such swindles in the mid- to late-19th century, many of them undiscovered because the victims never returned; however, occasionally one became known when the ship transporting them met some disaster and the fate of the Chinese passengers – or coolies – became known. What was revealed was the total callousness with which they had been treated, the brutalisation and absolute neglect. What is striking is the indifference with which the traders and the authorities regarded their passengers. There was no authority, Chinese or European, which exercised any control over the recruitment of labourers or the way they were treated.

One such case is that of the Peruvian sailing ship, the *Grimenza*, which sailed in May 1854 from Swatow (Shantou), known as a Chinese treaty port, meaning that it was open to trade with European and other foreign vessels. Her crew included the American captain John Penny and the Essex-born navigator William Collin, a 20-year-old seaman who had begun his life working on coal ships in England, but was gradually making his way to Australia, where he hoped to join the hunt for gold. The *Grimenza* offered him the opportunity to travel from Central America to the south Pacific, but first the captain needed to collect a number of Chinese workers and take them to lonely islands off the coast of South America, where they would start work digging guano, the dried excrement of sea-birds, which was greatly in demand as fertiliser. Guano was highly profitable for the exporters, but the unfortunate Chinese thought that they were being offered a passage to California, given the discovery of major goldfields there in 1849. California was booming, with great opportunities for immigrants, not only in the goldfields, but in agriculture, transport and trade.

Nor did anyone worry about the fact that the *Grimenza* was built to carry a maximum of 500 men, whereas the Chinese numbered more than 800. Within a few days, the cramped conditions, the overwhelming stench of their quarters below deck and the meagre food allowance they received led to growing unrest, all the more so when they began to realise that the route they were taking was not leading to California, but was far more southerly. Captain Penny was prepared for trouble, and he had a barricade set up by the mainmast to make sure that they could come up on deck only one man at a time. He also handed out weapons to those of his crew who were on duty. But trouble only grew and several Chinese fought their way beyond the barrier. He ordered them to be tied up and whipped before being flung back down below, with threats that any other troublemakers would be similarly treated and that leaders might be hanged. William Collin protested to the captain for this treatment, saying that they were not prisoners, but had paid for their passage, however modest the fee might have been. Penny ordered him back to work, but Collin refused to take part in any action which he might consider too brutal. It was something for which Penny would later make him pay.

Collin was off duty on 4 July when he felt the barque shudder and soon after come to a stop. They were sailing well off the coast of Queensland, passing through poorly charted waters and had struck Brampton Reef, some 800 kilometres from land. The screams of the Chinese and a quick survey revealed that the *Grimenza* was badly damaged, with water rapidly seeping into the hold. Penny ordered his crew to jump overboard and make for the beach. Collin was sent off with a couple of others to see if there was any food about, while the others prepared to man the boats. When he returned with a little fresh water and some fruits, he found that Penny had left in the larger boat with the doctor, the bosun and a few others, purposely leaving Collin to fend for himself and a dozen Peruvian and Chilean sailors. The problem was the screaming crowd of Chinese, trying to escape the fate of the 20 or 30 of them who had already drowned in the filthy bilge water down in the cracked keel, but at this stage there was nothing Collin could do for them. His one hope was a small boat suspended over the rear, dangling from the davits, in poor condition, but still better than nothing. He quickly had it lowered and rowed away in it, with the remaining sailors and what food supplies and water they could carry.

As for the Chinese coolies, he could do nothing for them. His own situation was desperate enough, as he struggled to keep to a westerly course that would bring him, hopefully, to the coast of Australia. Four days went by, with nothing in view, the food and the water running out, and the sailors becoming too weary and downhearted to keep on rowing. He led them as best he could, hope fading gradually, but on the ninth days one of the Chileans shouted the words they all hoped for – "Sail in sight!" But however hard they rowed, they had little hope of catching up a ship in sail. Fortunately, they were sighted and eventually rescued. Their saviour was the *Sophia*, which was on her way from Sydney to Calcutta but slowed down and helped them on board, generously altering course to take them to Blackwood Bay, near the present-day port of Mackay in northern Queensland.

It was here that they learnt of the eventual fate of the *Grimenza*. An American vessel in the bay, the *Eliza Warwick*, brought in a few Chinese survivors who told them that after Collin's departure, the seas had battered the wreck a little more, causing the mainmast to collapse, with the consequence that the *Grimenza*, now made lighter, drifted off the reef and began to float away. The Chinese threw overboard everything they could to lighten it further. Some of them constructed a rough type of raft with the broken masts and whatever planks they could find. Others worked on the remaining sails, mostly torn, tying them to whatever remained of the upper structures. This enabled the *Grimenza* to sail away, however awkwardly, for another two days, but then the water, which had continued to seep into the hold, caused the battered remnant of the ship to sink, drowning most of the surviving coolies. Some 20 of them managed to cling to the raft, which drifted slowly back to a small reef surrounded by a wide sandbank. There, they spent another eight to ten days, eating cockles but having no fresh water to drink. Luckily for the few who did not die of thirst or exhaustion, the *Eliza Warwick* came into view, noticed the men frantically waving from the shore, and brought them to Blackwood Bay.

As for Captain Penny and his supporters, he had struggled on towards New Guinea, reaching Rabaul after about 25 days. He had no means of returning to China or to Australia, but fortunately for him and his men, the *Australian*, a British ship, sailed into the bay and took them to Sydney. During this relatively short voyage, Penny fell out with his rescuer, Captain Wiles, and their dispute led to an informal enquiry into the wreck of the *Grimenza*. It proved inconclusive and no blame was attached to Penny – and no mention was made of the unfortunate Chinese, all but a handful of whom perished in a voyage they had never intended to make.

It was a time when no one felt any compassion for the Chinese or other Asians who met with neglect and misfortune while attempting to find work in the Pacific or along the west coast of America. Another example of this is the *Saint-Paul*, a French three-master from Nantes which sailed in August 1858 from Hong Kong, carrying 327 Chinese bound for the Australian goldfields. The fact that the ship was built for carrying cargoes and not passengers was of little importance to the owners or to the authorities who saw them off. The Chinese crowded together as best they could below deck, with a few crouching out of the way of the sailors in various corners of the top deck. They were prepared to suffer discomforts for a voyage that promised them a truly golden future. However, Captain Pinard had taken on insufficient food for a lengthy journey, as he expected the crossing to last a mere 40 or so days, and when he found himself held up by a series of weak breezes, he cut back on the daily rations, causing the Chinese to complain. He dealt with this by having their spokesmen shackled in irons as a warning to the rest and tried a new route close to New Guinea and the Solomon Islands. Buying a few coconuts and shells from nearby islanders who came out near the ship in their canoes was helpful, but insufficient for the Chinese whose rations were little improved and who continued to grumble among themselves.

He had hoped that sufficient winds would be blowing between New Guinea and Australia, but was proved wrong. The sea was rough, the currents unhelpful and a thick fog arose, which made it difficult to estimate his true location and his distance from the numerous islands that lie off the east end of New Guinea. He thought he was about to enter the Coral Sea, from which he

Two images depicting castaways from the Saint-Paul, *making for Rossel Island in 1858.*

could soon veer south towards Sydney, but he was far closer to the islands of the Louisiades than he thought. The *Saint-Paul* was still struggling along in the darkness during the early morning of 11 September 1858 when a sudden shock ran through the ship, bringing it to a standstill and causing all the crew and the terrified Chinese to run about the deck, shouting and desperately trying to find out what had happened. As daylight rose, it became clear that the *Saint-Paul* had struck a reef off some unknown island. They were in fact a short distance from Rossel Island, and were able to make their way to a small islet, Heron Island, the ship's longboat ferrying as many of the crew and the coolies as it could, the rest struggling their way across at low tide. They brought over as much of the food supplies and fresh water as they could until the *Saint-Paul* started to break up from the impact of the rising tide.

A few islanders appeared who were not unfriendly at first, even offering coconuts to the crowd of castaways. Captain Pinard established a camp on Rossel Island and started taking some of his men across. However, this was seen as a kind of invasion by the islanders, who attacked them in the morning. Eight men of his crew were killed, including his first officer, as well as an undisclosed number of Chinese. Pinard led a counter-attack, by way of reprisal, but also to reduce the islanders to some form of submission. He gathered his men for a discussion and it was agreed that the only hope was to seek help from Australia or any inhabited island. The Chinese were not consulted, although at a subsequent enquiry Pinard insisted that they had been and had agreed to the Europeans leaving in the boat to get help for them. Whether they were really told or understood his plan is not clear: they simply found out on the morning of 13 September that the boat was rowing away with the captain and 11 men.

They made their way towards the south. The weather was fine, which was helpful for the rowers who were helped by a small makeshift sail, but the heat became intolerable, especially in view of the small quantity of water they had with them. They mixed their flour with sea water to create a sort of broth to which they added the occasional floating leaves or dead fish they could scoop up. Twelve days went by, one of the sailors dying of exhaustion and being thrown overboard. They then reached Cape Flattery, on the north-easternmost point of Australia, not far from present-day Cooktown. The area was still unsettled, and the sailors were concerned about the presence of possibly hostile Aboriginals. They struggled along offshore, gathering shells and looking for fresh-water streams, on one occasion leaving behind the ship's boy, aged 14, who they thought might have got lost or been killed, but who in fact would manage to survive in the region for another 17 years.

After trying for three days to go south in the face of a steadily unfriendly breeze, Pinard decided to veer north, round Cape York into Torres Strait and seek help in Timor. On 5 October, they went ashore on a small island off Cape Greenville, 500 kilometres north of Flattery, collected shells and decided to sleep ashore, as they had done once or twice. In the morning, they found the longboat had been carried off and that they were prisoners of a tribal group. They were not ill-treated, although two more sailors died of exhaustion and sickness. A week later, they were rescued by a schooner, the *Prince of Denmark*, whose captain gave various gifts to the Aboriginals in exchange for their freedom and the return of the longboat. However, before worrying about rescuing the Chinese from Rossel Island, the captain continued his task of collecting tortoise shells, which he considered more important than looking for lost coolies. On 25 December, he finally dropped anchor in

New Caledonia, leaving Pinard and the surviving sailors to see what might be done, if anything, about the Chinese.

Captain Pinard went at once to the local authorities, made a full report on the loss of the *Saint-Paul*, and, presenting his own attitude as one of responsible humanity, appealed for help for the coolies. He was well received, and two days later the sloop *Styx*, with Pinard on board, steamed off in search of the possible survivors on Rossel Island. The steam-driven *Styx* wasted no time in making for Rossel and reached the island on 5 January. The French found the remains of the *Saint-Paul* and signs of the encampment, but none of the coolies, apart from two bodies buried under a heap of pebbles. They began a cautious search inland and along a small stream, and noticed some islanders watching them from two canoes; as the French came nearer, the islanders fled, but a man was found in the water, making silent gestures calling for help. He was a Chinese, and they brought him on board. He was naked and pleading for help, uttering only the words "All dead. All dead". Finally, he explained that the islanders had continually attacked the coolies, taking them away in small groups, killing them and, being cannibals, eating their bodies. However, he gave them to understand that four were still alive, prisoners working for their captors, but doomed to an eventual death.

The French began a cautious search for the survivors, endeavouring to negotiate with the islanders for their rescue, but they were constantly being pelted with stones and other missiles and realised that more islanders were creeping in the bush, endeavouring to surround the sailors for an eventual attack. The sailors found a small village, recently abandoned by the islanders, and everywhere remains of the dead coolies – bones, torn clothing, and worst of all scalps with the pigtails typical of the Chinese at the time.

Whenever they saw an islander, the French tried in vain to negotiate. Before long they gave up their efforts. There was a great deal of anger among the crew of the *Styx*, with calls for vengeance, but her captain, an officer called Grimoult, had received strict orders from his superiors to avoid any situation which might endanger the lives of his men. All he agreed to was to fire a few shots from the sloop's gun and burn down the huts. Then, he sailed for Sydney to refuel and to hand over the lone Chinese to the French consul in Sydney, which he did on 25 February. This provided Captain Pinard with the opportunity to make a final report on the disastrous voyage of the *Saint-Paul*.

Two more Chinese were rescued six years later by Captain Charles Edward of the schooner *Blue Bell*. They were sold to him as slaves by tribesmen of Peron Island, having apparently been previously sold to them by the islanders of Rossel. They cost Edward two hatchets. He took the men to Australia, where they had originally hoped to find work seven years earlier. Out of the original 327 coolies who had crowded into the *Saint-Paul*, only three had survived.

Neglect and ill-treatment resulting from the blackbirding trade or from the selfishness and avarice of the owners of trading vessels caused hardship and numerous deaths from the middle to late 19th century. However, as the years went by, Chinese and Indian immigrants settled in Australia, New Zealand and the Pacific Islands, successfully fossicking for gold, fishing, farming and trading. The price paid by their forerunners was a high one, but courage and determination did in the end lead to some worthwhile success.

12

Queen Emma Coe

The Pacific can claim two Queen Emmas who became famous in the late 19th century. One, Queen Emma of Hawaii, the wife of King Kamehameha IV, can be regarded as a real queen. The other, Queen Emma of Papua New Guinea, also known as Queen Emma of Samoa, was a part-European woman of great beauty, a skilful and dominating trader, who could lay claim to some form of Samoan nobility as a princess in the Moli tribe of Samoa.

Her father was an American trade representative and dealer named Jonas Myndersee Coe who was living in what was known as American Samoa. She was born in September 1850 in Apia, and her parents endeavoured to do their best for her, making sure that she had a good education and that her manners fitted in with what they saw as the coming European or American Pacific world. In 1869, she married an officer from an American merchant vessel, James Forsayth (or Forsyth), and together they set up a shipping and trading venture. Whether this was a love match or arranged by her parents to ensure her future in the developing world is not easy to determine, but early portraits of Emma Coe show an attractive and well-dressed young woman, closer to European fashions than to island style, while her father is known to have built major links with the authorities and worked to promote his own position on the island.

However, James Forsayth was lost at sea in 1872, leaving the young widow in sole charge of their trading enterprise. Using her charms as well as her business skills, Emma continued to build up her company. She became closely linked with Colonel Steinberger, a special agent of the American government in Apia. He is described as a man of some charm and intelligence who sought to manoeuvre his way between the various factions of the time, British, American and German, which were involved in a complex and often bitter struggle to impose their power over the area, a situation complicated by the actions of the missionaries, Catholic and Protestant, and of the various islander clans. In 1876 Steinberger was finally expelled from Samoa, as was Jonas Coe, and went to Fiji. Emma saw no reason to follow him there, however romantically attached she may have been to him, and he eventually gave up his struggles and returned to the United States. Emma Coe-Forsyth had a business to defend against those who resented her links with someone who was regarded as a foreign agent, and she stayed behind, looking forward to some new and safer associate.

This turned out to be Thomas James Farrell, an Australian merchant of Irish descent who was known as an often unscrupulous trader, a blackbirder, but certainly as someone who knew the region, sailing constantly from one isolated island to another, in search of goods and also recruiting island labour. She sailed with him to parts of New Britain and New Ireland to the east of Papua New Guinea. They were attracted by the small island of Mioko, in the Duke of York group of the Bismarck archipelago, as yet undeveloped and offering good possibilities for copra plantations.

Queen Emma of Hawaii at the start of the 1880s.

Farrell was not keen to settle, preferring to continue trading among the islands, but the political situation in Samoa made it necessary for Emma to leave Apia. Selling her business, she moved to New Britain in October 1878. They had agreed that they could set up a plantation, but that Farrell could continue his trading among the islands.

Calling themselves Mr and Mrs Farrell, they settled on Mioko. They were joined by one of Emma's brothers and a few Samoans. While Thomas Farrell went off on his usual trading and blackbirding operations, Emma started work on Mioko, buying land from the locals and reselling some of it to new arrivals, dealing with passing merchantmen in copra and coconuts, and, on occasion, dealing firmly with aggressive islanders. In 1880, they helped settlers marooned after the failure of the infamous Marquis de Rays' plan to develop a "New France" in New Ireland to make their way to Australia. In so doing, they bought cheaply – or simply picked up – items brought by the French for their supposed settlement: knives, tools, bricks and cement. They even obtained a slab of white marble that some pious colonists had intended to use as an altar for a chapel that was of course never built – it served as a bar in the Farrells' home.

Emma was an energetic and skilled woman, determined to get her own way and expecting obedience and respect from her followers. Her "husband" clearly admired her talents and her success, and he cut back on his expeditions around the islands to help her and give added strength to her position, especially when she bought land and developed a new estate in Kokopo, in eastern New Guinea. This enabled them to broaden their range of activities and assert themselves in a district as yet uncolonised. They threw parties for visiting trading ships and for the locals who included a number of German settlers. It was during this period of growth and enrichment that she became known as "Queen Emma of New Guinea". Commercially, from 1880 to 1890, her business enterprises dominated the region, and her influence was undeniable. But there were ongoing colonial manoeuvres, with several European countries endeavouring to assert themselves in the islands and in Papua New Guinea.

This presented a threat of sorts to Emma Coe, with her Samoan background and her associations with British and American traders. She decided to use these to build up a form of defence for her business. Using her marital links, she claimed some form of American citizenship, and used the American consul in Sydney to formally recognise her purchases of land. She laid further claims to British protection when Thomas Farrell died of tuberculosis in 1886, strengthening her position when the Germans began to establish their colony in north-eastern New Guinea. But obtaining German protection, as usual through her womanly charms, was important, and she became associated with a German officer of Dalmatian origin, Agostino Stalio, with whom she purchased a property in the Rabaul district.

Surrounded by members of her family and business associates, she continued to lead a stylish life, impressing all around her. She was described on one occasion by a visiting trader as a lady of great bearing, "with a tiara adorned with diamonds resting upon her flowing dark hair, wearing a long dress of white satin with a train carried by a dozen small island boys dressed in a variety of baroque costumes". This did not mean that life in the region was safe for all, especially not for those who were engaged in trading and blackbirding. In 1892, her brother John was killed during a raid on the isolated atoll of Nuguria. An expedition was organised to avenge this crime, but the islanders were on their guard, and this time it was Stalio who was killed by a skilfully hurled spear. Once more alone, Emma continued her trading and plantation work, erecting a memorial to Stalio on their property in Gunantambu. But she needed to strengthen her position yet again in the growing German colony. She was now 43, and her beauty was beginning to fade, affected not just by the passing years, but by occasional bouts of fever.

She still had enough charm and presence to follow her practice of attracting men of influence. And what she may have lost in physical beauty, she could make up in personal appeal, gracious manners and, above all, money. She turned her attention to a German official, a former officer in the Prussian cavalry, August Karl Paul Kolbe. He could ensure her entry into the German aristocracy or at least into the influential world of colonial administrators, while she could bring him wealth and status. They travelled to Sydney where they were married in 1893. Emma Kolbe decided to make her way back to Apia, in order to impress her old acquaintances and her relatives. She could now display herself as Queen Emma of Samoa, entertain in her grand style, and at the same time endow some of her relations with a share of her wealth.

Paul Kolbe was somewhat shocked at the way his wife showed herself in Samoan society, and seemed in no hurry to return to Rabaul. A Hungarian visitor, Count Festetics de Tolna, a friend of the British novelist Robert Louis Stevenson, has left a somewhat critical portrait of Emma during their stay in Apia: "Princess Emma, that is how they refer to a certain Madam Kolbe, a half-breed of Samoa descent who behaves in New Pomerania like a kind of Pompadour combined with a colonial Mrs Humbert. She is the one who pulls all the strings in the colonial administration and in order to keep under her thumb the company's employees and the colonial magistrates, she maintains a *parc aux cerfs* [Madame de Pompadour's quarters in Louis XV's Versailles] consisting of kanaka girls whose pretty eyes can grant anything one wishes. Mrs Kolbe, a first-class business woman, can thus make excellent profits through the complicity of the authorities and build up an immense fortune".

Always planning to ensure that she was not caught out by unexpected developments, Emma kept an eye on the international situation and the growing rivalry among the European powers in the Pacific and elsewhere. She sensed that a conflict would drive Germany out of the region, and feared that, having acquired German nationality through her marriage to Kolbe, she might lose her position and her wealth. Alternatively, if she succumbed to whatever illness was causing her occasional bouts of fever, she worried that Kolbe might inherit her fortune and neglect her family. In 1909, she handed over one of her plantations to her son Jonas, made several donations to other relatives, and sold the balance of her land holdings and trading businesses to a German company for a neat one million American dollars. She then moved to Sydney, together with her husband who was himself in poor health. They had somewhat drifted apart in recent years. Kolbe kept it to himself, but her ruthless trading methods, her manipulations of officials and other traders, her general behaviour among the locals, had embarrassed him and it is plain that they had argued on a number of occasions. Living in Sydney brought the matter to a head, and in 1911 he left for Europe and settled in Monte Carlo.

Emma remained in Australia for a while, but she lacked the status she had come to expect, and her own health was deteriorating. She was now in her sixties, and she felt isolated and bored, and when news arrived from Europe that Paul Kolbe was now seriously ill, she decided to join him in Monte Carlo. He died there on 19 July 1913, and she survived him for only a couple of days.

She had made arrangements for them to be buried together back in Gunantambu. Their ashes were taken for an official burial, with a commemorative plaque. A mere few yards away lay the remains of Captain Stalio. Then the First World War broke out, and the German colony was taken over by Australian and British forces.

13

James Proctor
"Captain One-Leg", Blackbirder

As the Pacific area became the target for more European trade and development, the demand for labour grew. Australia welcomed new settlers, but also needed additional workers to open up new regions for farming. In northern Queensland, for instance, cotton and sugar cane plantations could be developed if enough labour was available. In the islands, there was a welcome growth in copra, especially in Samoa; while in New Caledonia, nickel mines offered new possibilities if manpower could be found. Locals were at times tempted to assist, but they had links with their own district, and were reluctant to leave for another life, especially as they had no means of returning home if the need arose.

From the early 1860s, the first recruiting vessels appeared in the Pacific islands. "Labour ships", as they were called, sailing among the Solomon Islands, the Marquesas, the New Hebrides, as Vanuatu was then called, and other island groups, offering so-called contracts, which promised work in some other territory, with the implied promise of repatriation after three years. The Queensland administration had even appointed an agent to ensure that no one was recruited without their consent, and a form was prepared with an official seal to be signed or marked with his thumbprint by the islander. In fact, what happened in most cases was that the islanders were lured on board and distracted while the ship raised anchor and sailed off to another destination.

An estimated 70,000 young men and women are understood to have been taken from the Vanuatu area between 1866 and 1890. Some 48,000 Pacific islanders, mostly from the Solomons and Papua New Guinea, are believed to have been brought to work in Queensland. Thousands of Melanesians were sent to work in the Fiji group. Many died in transit or on plantations from illnesses and ill-treatment. Blackbirding became a regular and much feared feature of island life.

Not surprisingly, these practices soon aroused the enmity of the islanders and there were a number of serious incidents in which innocent traders or missionaries were attacked. The most famous case was that of the Anglican bishop John Patterson who was killed on the island of Nukapu in the Solomons in September 1871 as reprisals for the kidnapping of islanders by a blackbirder. The British government tried to put an end to this dangerous situation by passing the Pacific Islanders Protection Act of 1872, sometimes called the "Kidnapping Act", but enforcing it was difficult. Patrolling such a vast area was almost impossible, and identifying the true blackbirders from ordinary small merchantmen was even more difficult. The efforts of the British and Australian authorities may have had some effect, but some of the blackbirders were too ruthless and crafty to cope with.

One of the most famous of these was an American, James Toutant Proctor. He was born in 1846 in Louisiana where his parents ran a vast estate with over 200 slaves, growing maize and sugar cane. The family had also a military background: his uncle Toutant Beauregard was a general. James had enrolled at the local military college in Alexandria, and when the American Civil War broke out at the end of 1860, James joined the rebel forces. But in May 1863, when he was still only 17, he lost his right leg at the battle of Chancellorsville in Virginia. Once he had sufficiently recovered, he joined his uncle in South Carolina and was one of the delegation appointed to negotiate the surrender of the southern troops with General William T. Sherman.

The war and the abolition of slavery that followed it almost ruined his parents. There was no future for him in what remained of their plantations, and he began a brief career as a lawyer. But he still dreamt of ruling an estate as his family had done, and he felt that this might be a possibility somewhere in the Pacific islands. Fiji seemed promising, and in 1870 he sailed for Melbourne where he discussed his plans with the American consul who happened to own a cotton plantation in Fiji. He then left for Suva to see for himself what might be available. The information he obtained satisfied him and he returned to Australia to obtain the supplies he felt were needed for his enterprise. In Sydney, he bought plant, food and other supplies and two horses, all of which he loaded onto the schooner *Kestrel*. Unfortunately, the ship was wrecked in a storm and the two horses and most of the material he had brought with him were lost. This did not stop him from developing land near the Ba River on Viti Levu. He is reported as ruling his estate as if he was still a slave owner in old Louisiana, and on at least two occasions he is known to have shot some Fijians, one because he annoyed him by trying to sell him a turtle shell which Europeans were known to treasure. Not surprisingly, there were reprisals by islanders. Two settlers were murdered by rebellious Fijians, and in August 1871

Proctor, on horseback, led a small army of Melanesians and settlers that burned down several villages and ravaged the countryside.

However, his cotton plantation did not prosper, and he decided to try his luck in the Californian goldfields. He was not successful there either and made his way back to Louisiana. He saw no future in the post-slavery world and by 1875 he was back in the Pacific, determined to make his money by trading rather than farming. Based firstly in Rotuma, Fiji, he moved to the islands of Wallis and Futuna, ruled by the French who knew very little of his background and were less likely to interfere with his plans, which consisted not simply of dealing in copra, but in recruiting labour for distant settlements. Finding islanders willing to embark for the supposed three-year contract was not easy, and he resorted to a number of tricks which increased his reputation as a crafty and unscrupulous kidnapper. On many occasions, he would invite islanders to board his schooner and share a meal or collect some payment for the fish or coconuts they were trying to sell him. Then, he would sink their canoes and sail away, keeping them below decks under armed guard. At other times, he would entice them with a display of his artificial leg, keeping them amused until his sailors gathered around them with guns and forced them aboard. But straightforward kidnapping was his usual method.

Not surprisingly, his reputation grew and worried the authorities, especially the French missionaries. His kidnapping of a young girl in Futuna, whom he intended to keep for himself, brought about an argument during which Proctor adopted his normal stance of drawing out his revolver and firing it indiscriminately. The French authorities placed him under arrest, but his skill in talking himself out of awkward situations soon put an end to the dispute. However, he moved soon after to the island of Mallicollo (or Malekula, in the

New Hebrides) where he cleared land for a small settlement, with 50 Melanesian labourers – naturally unpaid – who worked for him, while he lived in a well-defended, palisaded house.

Combining his work as a planter, trader and kidnapper made it easier for him to evade the authorities. If he was met by a British or French ship, he would draw attention to his stocks of copra and other goods, which he used as evidence that all he was doing was trading between various islands. Nor did he have problems with planters and station owners to whom he offered the unfortunate islanders he had on board. All he was doing, he told them, was to provide them with transport to places where they hoped to find work, and all he wanted was a sum to cover his costs, including their accommodation and food, which he said was to be deducted from their first three or six months' wages. He therefore could not be accused of slave trading or blackbirding: all he was doing was helping the islanders to find work. Getting his money back by receiving funds from the planters was a straightforward and honest procedure.

He was a skilled negotiator, a man with a reputation as an American military officer, with a strong and dominating personality. The various authorities he dealt with at times, whether British, French or American, were usually impressed by him and hesitated to credit the various rumours they heard about his brutality and his moral insensitivity. Only the missionaries doubted him, because they often were nearer to the islanders than the various consuls and administrative officers, and they heard first-hand reports about his actions, but their influence on the other residents of the region was limited.

The French journalist and author Jules Durand who met him in the 1880s describes the power of his personality: "He had eyes of

James Proctor playing his prosthetic leg to great advantage with the Melanesians.

steel, a fine moustache, a lithe body and the cool and quiet manner of speaking of an upright man that nothing can upset and who feels that he is carrying out his mission." In a book published some years later, *Bois d'Ebene* (Ebony Wood), Durand quotes a comment of Proctor's that better expresses the cynicism of the man: "In the strange profession that I am following, one needs to be cautious, cool and collected. How many times have I been followed by armed vessels! I could have been seen as some low-born buccaneer, and hanged as soon as captured. But I saw to it that I behaved in an irreproachable manner, and my perfect behaviour saved me even in the worst circumstances".

A favoured trick of his was to land on some island and lay out a display of items he was prepared to offer the inhabitants. While they examined them, he would sit under some tree, smoke his pipe and relax. Then he would ask one of the younger men to help him take off his boots. He first of all offered his left leg, which presented no problem; then his right one which proved more difficult until, all of a sudden, the entire leg would come off. All the islanders were appalled. Proctor would retrieve his leg, but insist on them paying some compensation, either for the insult which he claimed had been inflicted on him or, if the circumstances permitted it, the hurt his body had suffered. Compensation would be in the form of four or five men who were taken on board, to be sold to some settler on another island.

On one occasion, in Port Resolution, on the island of Tanna, his trick almost cost him his artificial leg, when a local, having taken off Proctor's boot and finding his leg in it, fled with it into the bush. It took some hours before Proctor and his men caught up with him. He was able to enforce a satisfactory retribution, claiming not only an insult to his person, but the possibility of magic powers associated with it leading to some evil consequences for the entire tribe, which could only be avoided by a number of islanders coming to serve him on board.

He set up trading posts on various islands, associated with various American, French or British firms. He was known to change over to various schooners, renaming them and flying different flags, thus confusing the authorities. In the mid-1880s, he worked for a while with a German company, but his reputation as an unscrupulous blackbirder led them to sever relations with him. Some years later, he became manager of a branch of the Australian New Hebrides Company in Port Vila, but is believed to have traded for his own account at the same time. Arguing with him was unwise and dangerous, and on two occasions he is reported as having fired on islanders and even having killed one of his own employees. He was arrested for this murder and taken to Fiji, but the American consul helped him argue, as his defence, that Port Vila was outside British jurisdiction and that he could only be judged by an American tribunal, if at all. Proctor was consequently freed, but agreed that it would unwise for him to return to the New Hebrides. Consequently, in January 1893, we find him in Auckland in New Zealand, considering the possibility of resuming his trading work in the south-west Pacific.

He decided against this, feeling that his situation in the Pacific was becoming too dangerous, and he sailed for the United States. By September, he was back in Louisiana. The political situation was now easing, and he joined the association of civil war veterans, re-entering society and boasting of his years as a trader and plantation owner in the Pacific. No rumours of his behaviour as a brutal blackbirder seem to have reached Louisiana. He was now 47, his parents and his uncle were dead, and he had no close relatives left. Two years after his return, he married a wealthy widow whom he had known in his youth. They lived in comfort in New Orleans, while regretting their earlier years when slavery and tradition had ensured they could enjoy a status which the social reforms and the abolitionist policies of the new world had now undermined.

Nevertheless, Proctor was able to find his way into the new administration. He had a cousin who was a judge in the state's Supreme Court, and through him obtained a position in the legal administration. It might sound ironic that a man who had several times been accused of crimes, including murder, and who had escaped prosecution by claiming that he should be judged only by American authorities, was now working in the judicial system, holding a position which he felt confident would open the way for him to acquire even greater status.

Unfortunately, his health had suffered over the year from attacks of malaria and other tropical illnesses, and in part through excessive drinking. He died at the age of 54. An obituary published in a local paper made no mention of his shady past, since rumours of his blackbirding had not reached New Orleans. Instead, he was described as "A quiet man, and like all brave men, he was very modest and discreet".

14

Charles de Rays, King of Oceania

The French Revolution of 1789 struck at the aristocracy which had ruled France for centuries, and not surprisingly destroyed the prospects of most of its members. For one young man, gloriously named Charles Bonaventure du Breil de Rays, who was born in Brittany in 1832, the world in which his ancestors had enjoyed power and wealth had long since gone. Worse, he lived through his youth to see the monarchy, which had been restored after the fall of Napoleon, overthrown in 1848, when Charles was 16, and replaced by a republic, and three years later by the second empire.

He inherited from his father the castle of Quimerch in western Brittany, but it was old and costly to maintain. What he dreamt of was finding wealth and some form of power, as his ancestors had enjoyed. The hope of discovering a goldmine, as others were reported to have done, led him to the United States. He failed, so moved on to Africa, trying his hand as a trader in Senegal, again with little luck. His next attempt was in the East, travelling around

Thailand, but still with nothing that promised fortune and status.

Back in France, he approached the new emperor, Napoleon III, seeking an appointment as a trading representative of France in the island of Madagascar. This got him nowhere. Looking at the map, he saw vast supposedly empty and unclaimed stretches of land in western Australia and devised a plan to create a French colony there. This proposal was promptly banned by the British authorities, and a similar plan to create a semi-independent agricultural colony in New Caledonia was quickly

Charles de Rays, pedlar of dreams.

ended by the French government, which was determined to govern the whole island without interference from a royalist entrepreneur. By 1878, Charles de Rays was almost ruined, but still driven by dreams of a distant empire that would bring him wealth and fame.

He studied the map of the Pacific, which French and British explorers had by now clarified, and was attracted by the narrative of Louis Duperrey, which drew his attention to the attractive scenery and climate of places such as New Guinea and New Ireland. The major European powers were setting up trading posts and colonies in the region, and it occurred to him that he could create his own kingdom in the area. He drew a map of an area he named New France, which included New Ireland and a substantial part of New Guinea and the Solomon Islands. The task that now faced him was to turn this dream into a reality.

However, now in his mid-forties, he had no intention of leading an expedition to these distant and still relatively unexplored territories. He had created a kingdom for himself, which he would rule to the extent this was possible from Paris or some other suitable European city. He had published a small brochure advertising his attempt to settle part of western Australia, but he now decided on a far more impressive strategy: he held a public meeting in Marseilles, which resulted in the creation of several companies, the "Company of Farmers of New France" as well as subsidiary companies dealing with trade, sugar refining and mining.

He reached a wider public by publishing a periodical, *La Nouvelle France*, subtitled *Journal de la Colonie Libre de Port-Breton en Oceanie*. The first issue appeared in mid-July 1879 and continued to appear on a more or less monthly basis for seven years. This not only ensured that he would become known among the leaders

The Chandernagor *leaving the port of Le Havre in 1879 was forced to fly the American flag due to the French government's objections to its voyage.*

of Europe as the king and eventually as the emperor Charles I of Oceania, but also gather supporters among the French and even among the Italians and the Spanish. His aim, as he worked on his dream map of the south-western Pacific, was to send settlers and administrators to these distant territories, but above all to sell them parts of the land which he now claimed as his. Buyers in fact would not need to leave France – they could, if they chose, remain in France as investors. The land they had purchased would soon rise in value – for who could not wish that their ancestors had invested in land in North America so that they could now, from the comfort of Paris or London, watch its value rise while the hard-working settlers continued to farm, trade or mine in what had become Canada and the United States?

Hence, he advertised in the daily newspaper *Le Petit Parisien* offering land at five francs a hectare in the "Free Colony of Port

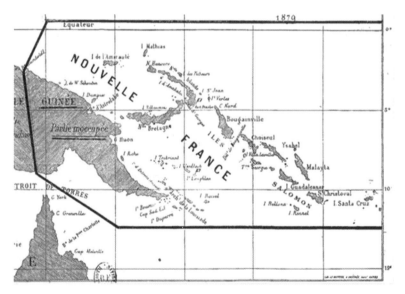

Map of Nouvelle France.

Breton" which would ensure "a prompt and safe fortune to be made without leaving one's country". To encourage investors, he created an order of New France nobility, which was linked to the amount one invested. In this, he tried to link his enterprise with the royalist sentiment which had survived several revolutions. "The idea of our free colony", he wrote in the *Nouvelle France*, "was born out of a patriotic and religious feeling... Alas, poor fatherland, what has become of your glory? Eldest daughter of the church, where is your crown?"

Not surprisingly, people supported his scheme. Those who began as mere investors saw the price of the land rise to 15 francs a hectare – a 300% profit for them – and in a third issue to an absurd 50 francs. The marquis was hailed wherever he toured and at last found himself wealthy and honoured. Meanwhile, the first settlers had readied themselves for a new life in the distant promised land. The merchant ship *Chandernagor* was prepared to take 80 settlers to their new home. However, the French government was not willing to support the plan and warned that anyone endeavouring to build a colony without its formal authority could be prosecuted. The *Chandernagor* was forbidden to fly the French flag and it seemed likely that the officials in the port of Le Havre, where the ship was anchored, might step in and put a stop to the project. Consequently, the captain decided to leave France without delay and make for the port of Antwerp, in Belgium, where he could make his final arrangements and obtain the supplies he would need for the long voyage. He sailed on 14 September 1879 with the 80 would-be settlers, flying the American colours. This was changed to a Liberian ensign, because the American consul in Madeira, where the *Chandernagor* made a brief call, protested and threatened to have him arrested if he insisted on using the Stars and Stripes.

The expedition reached its final destination, a bay in New Ireland, at the end of January 1880. What had been hailed as a South Seas paradise turned out to be a marshy area surrounded by densely forested hills. Rumours that huts would be found awaiting the new arrivals were proved to be as false as much of the publicity that had surrounded the launching of the commercial enterprise. There was hardly a path to be found that might lead to some area where some form of farming could be undertaken. Coconut and banana trees might be planted once the winding weeds were cleared, but it would take years for them to flourish and there was no real market for them accessible in the region. There was nothing welcoming in this New France, apart from mosquitoes, ants and, as some suspected, lurking islanders watching the strange new arrivals from the jungle.

But the *Chandernagor* needed to sail back to France, and the captain literally pushed the migrants ashore and sailed away. What really happened to them from day to day is not clear. They had a few supplies, and tools to try and build some huts; they fished and

The reality of life in New Ireland that greeted the new settlers.

hunted for nuts and anything they could eat in the bush, suffering from the heat and insect bites. A handful tried to get away, but were caught by local Papuans and all but one were never seen again. Some 30 men died of various illnesses or drowning, but approximately 50 eventually succeeded in making their way to Australia. A dozen stayed back and were cheered by the return of the so-called Governor, a man named Titeu de la Croix, who brought a supply of bricks and tools with him, including some very welcome foodstuffs. He had hoped to build a house or fort which, in time, would be the centre of the colony; but it was soon clear to him that there was neither enough labour, nor enough spirit, for the work to be done. So, on 25 August 1880, the settlement was abandoned, and the few survivors in their turn made their way to Australia.

They had no way of knowing that a second expedition was on its way. Within a few days after their departure, the ship *Genil* put in to the bay, but it had little to offer, as all the would-be colonists who had sailed from Europe had long since deserted. There had been only 28 of them, mostly of Spanish origin, who had fallen out with the captain, a man named Rabardy, described as a paranoid brute who was so afraid of his crew and passengers that he dined and slept with a revolver close at hand. The Spaniards had deserted at Aden; they had been replaced by Arabs who walked off when the *Genil* called at Sri Lanka and at Singapore, and what Captain Rabardy now brought to New France was a mixed group of 25, most of whom he needed to replace some of his own crew who had left a ship where life seemed totally chaotic. There was, however, a third vessel on its way to Port Breton, the *India*, for which Rabardy decided to wait while his men rested and fearfully explored what they had been told was already a settlement.

The *India* arrived on 14 October, bringing supplies and 340

This illustration, drawn for the Sydney Mail *of October 1880, depicts two parts of the rough and ready settlement prepared for the potential colonists of New Ireland. To show the contrast between de Rays' promises and reality, a view of an immigrant ship is superimposed on the huts roughly put together for the settlers.*

would-be settlers, a large number of whom were Italians with wives and children. The publicity de Rays had spread through his *Nouvelle France* had included drawings of the settlement which he claimed had by now been built and developed by the earlier migrants. The crossing from Europe had been uncomfortable due to overcrowding and illnesses which had claimed the lives of six children. And what the new migrants found on arrival was as depressing as it could be, particularly for those who had invested their money to buy what had been described as a Promised Land, where they could develop farms and large estates. They saw nothing but a narrow strip of muddy land, a seemingly impenetrable jungle, and dark hills all around. In addition to which, it rained in tropical downpours for the first three days. The new "governor", an able man named Le Prevost, agreed with Rabardy that he should sail as promptly as possible to Sydney in the *Genil*, obtain supplies and return to finally develop a liveable colony.

Le Prevost left as promptly as he could and arrived safely in Sydney. He found the authorities quite unsympathetic, and the French consul even more so. They had by now received enough bad reports from the so-called settlement of Port Breton, some from the would-be settlers who had managed to get away from it, to suspect that the entire enterprise was based on lies. Le Prevost nevertheless struggled to obtain funds, supported by a credit line previously arranged by the Marquis de Rays, and buy clothing, tools, utensils of various types and a small supply of building bricks and tiles. He was keen to return to Port Breton – he had promised to do so within two months – but the *Genil* was in need of repairs and the strain he found himself under caused him to suffer a heart attack. A missionary and one Henri Niau, who had invested thousands of francs in de Rays' company, took over and they eventually sailed for Port Breton.

By then, unfortunately, the settlers had given up and the *India* had sailed a few days earlier, intending to find a safe haven somewhere in Australia. The voyage, however, was too difficult without new supplies and the ship struggled on to Noumea, in New Caledonia, where it did manage to obtain supplies of fresh water and, above all, medicine to counter the fevers from which most of the 200 passengers and crew were suffering. The French colonists in Noumea had donated enough money and supplies to help them, and an article in the newspaper *Le Neo-Caledonien*, of 18 March 1881, describes how the condition of the passengers of the *India* had caused so much pity that the colonists' generosity was understandable:

"The first impression one gets on climbing on board is the state of misery one comes across. Here are mothers holding in their arms a baby yellow with fever who refuses any kind of food. Over there are people so sick they can hardly stand. Others are lying down on a rough bed, suffering and ready to follow their comrades whom death has already carried away. All this gives rise to feelings of deep pity."

Some of the passengers, about 15 Italians, decided to find a home in New Caledonia. The rest went on to Australia where they finally succeeded in settling. The Italians mostly stayed together and created a small colony in New South Wales sometimes referred to as "Little Italy". There are today Australians who can claim to be descendants of the victims of the Marquis de Rays' crooked plans.

He had made a great deal of money from his scheme, but he would not escape final punishment. The reports that were reaching the French authorities added to the complaints of investors who now discovered that they had purchased non-existent tracts of land in a region which was little known and often misrepresented. In June 1882, a warrant was issued for de Rays' arrest. He had moved to Spain, so steps had to be taken by the French authorities for his extradition, a move the Spanish authorities were quite willing to support.

The trial began in Paris at the beginning of 1884. Evidence was brought showing that the accused had collected the equivalent of more than a million and a half modern euros, only a quarter of which had been spent on the various expeditions. The marquis had lied and appeared to have fooled even his closest friends; however, as the prosecution soon proved, these friends knew what was going on and had skimmed off their own slice of the profits.

The marquis was sentenced to six years' jail and a fine of 3,000 francs. His associates received sentences of between six and eight months. His lawyer, a man called Chambaud, was sentenced to 12 months, but he had already fled the country. The prosecution stated that these sentences were relatively mild, considering that so many investors had lost their savings and over 300 would-be colonists had died of starvation, illness or drowning. A charge of manslaughter had originally been added to the other accusations laid against de Rays, but it was dropped, being too difficult to prove, considering the distance and the lack of firm evidence.

De Rays served his sentence in full in the Mazas prison in Paris, then moved back to Brittany, spending a few years in a manor house at Bannelec, but he eventually undertook a lengthy voyage overseas in the *Tyburnia*, visiting several countries, but avoiding the south-west Pacific islands where he had once dreamt of creating his own empire. Far from having made his fortune, he was adjudged bankrupt in 1888 and his small chateau of Bannelec was sold by his creditors. He struggled on for a few years, dying on 29 July 1893, aged 61. His memory endured as a cross between a crook and a fool, and his character was used by the novelist Alphonse Daudet in his novel *Port-Tarascon: Dernières Aventures de L'Illustre Tartarin*, and by the novelist and playwright Jules Romains in a play, *Donogoo-Tonka*.

15

Count Von Attems

The numerous colonies and outposts of the Pacific world offered great opportunities to crooks and others who wanted to impress the settlers and create a position for themselves. The townships and ports were relatively isolated, and the means of communication with Europe, America and other settlements were slow and often difficult. International banking hardly existed, so that businessmen and government officials usually accepted bills of exchange drawn by the client – a situation not uncommon in the rest of the world at the time.

Therefore, when men arrived in a settlement, dressed in an imposing manner and referring to important people back in their home countries as close acquaintances or even relatives, the locals could hardly fail to be impressed. This was the case of a youngish man who landed in Sydney in 1867, staying at the Royal Hotel, and claiming to be Count Von Attems, a member of a highly regarded aristocratic Prussian family. Sydney, however, was a little overcrowded for his purpose, as he feared meeting someone who actually knew his true identity. He decided to move north to Brisbane, planning to make his way to the more promising – and possibly safer – Dutch East Indies.

He bought, or hired, a small schooner, cleverly named the *Hamlet's Ghost*, having been built out of the remains of another shipwrecked schooner called *The Prince of Denmark*. He cut a fine figure among the residents: "his beard carefully trimmed and anointed with pomade, dressed in the latest London style, he strode about in his high Wellington boots, visiting local cafés and saloons. Claiming to be a member of the Prussian nobility, Count Von Attems, followed by a small attendant, had a great presence. Caressing his golden beard with fingers adorned with rings, he fascinated his audience. With the ladies, he talked constantly about his hunting expeditions in Africa and in India and the hundreds of occasions when he had risked his life. He seemed to possess great wealth, but he paid most of his accounts by drawing bills of exchange. This is what he did when he purchased the *Hamlet's Ghost* for five hundred pounds".

He recruited a captain and three sailors, and sailed down the river on a trial run by which the locals were duly impressed. Unfortunately, he thought that his departure would be enhanced by firing a salute from one of the small guns carried by the schooner. It exploded, inflicting some facial wounds on Von Attems, forcing him to return for some moderate medical treatment. He also fell out with the captain and appointed a new one, named Howes, telling him to sail along the coast and on to northern Queensland where he was to meet a Prussian-owned ship, transfer to it and thus make his way back to the Dutch East Indies and on to Europe.

It was now July 1868. The *Hamlet's Ghost* set off, but the captain and one of the sailors were unhappy when Von Attems suggested that it would be preferable to make their way to New Caledonia, as he felt confident the Prussian vessel would call there and stay awhile, discussing political and trade matters with the French authorities. The sailor, McQuade, became quite angry and pointed out that the small vessel lacked supplies for such a journey and sailing on would mean making their way to certain death. The captain was equally uneasy. He had realised that Von Attems knew very little about the problems of navigation, especially in the vast and ill-charted Pacific Ocean. They made their way cautiously up the coast, calling at Maryborough, 250 kilometres north of Brisbane, where McQuade was sacked and left ashore to seek the services of a lawyer who helped him to make a claim against Von Attems for six months' wages. He eventually won, but getting the money was another matter, as the tradespeople back in Brisbane were beginning to discover with their own unpaid bills, and by the time McQuade obtained the judgement he wanted, the *Hamlet's Ghost* had sailed north to Bowen, almost 1,000 kilometres away and well out of touch.

Bowen was a small settlement, enjoying the benefits of a rich alluvial soil and good opportunities for fishing, but it had but few inhabitants and there was no sign of any Prussian vessel. Captain Howes had grown increasingly worried about Von Attems' claims and he confided his misgivings to the local government representative, Jardine. However, Jardine was himself but a recent settler and more concerned about developing his own land than about the plans of some strange German visitor. There was little Jardine could have done in any case, and he kept out of what seemed to him little more than an argument between a ship's master and his employer. He could not fail anyhow to be impressed by Von Attems' attire, particularly by his Wellington boots and what seemed to be medals from several foreign countries. He entertained Von Attems to dinner, listened to his tales about his travels, and provided him with supplies for the next stage of his journey, paid as it turned out by one of the Count's valueless bills of exchange.

Captain Howes refused to go any further, and Von Attems appointed in his stead a sailor named Austen, who had considerable experience, including sailing through the Solomon Islands in the *Alliance*, which had unfortunately sunk on some coral reef, forcing Austen to hitch his way home by accepting any job he could find. As it turned out, Austen was an able sailor who took the *Hamlet's Ghost* safely north to the Dutch East Indies, with the first port of call being Surabaya on the island of Java.

Von Attems had left a note for the captain of the Prussian vessel, asking Jardine to hand it to him when he finally arrived. It told the Prussians that Von Attems was planning to make his way to Timor, where he would await his arrival. He also gave other letters to be sent on to Sydney, some addressed to bankers there, dealing, as he explained to Jardine, with the financial arrangements he had made during his stay in Australia. Jardine could hardly fail to be impressed by these actions, and he felt quite satisfied about the bill Von Attems had given him for the supplies loaded on board.

When the *Hamlet's Ghost* dropped anchor in Surabaya, Von Attems put on his usual impressive gear, as carefully ironed as was possible on the schooner, and called on the authorities, announcing his presence and his plans, but also complaining that a British merchantman had failed to salute the Prussian flag which now adorned his small ship. It was explained to him that the merchant ship, the schooner *Diamond*, was on an official mission for the Dutch authorities, bringing a consignment of horses for the local cavalry, and had no doubt felt that its status was superior to the smaller *Hamlet's Ghost*. Nevertheless, the locals were duly impressed by the Count and, for several days, entertained him at their homes and paid him the respect he felt was his due.

Unfortunately for him, he was soon to be unmasked, and his fall was to be totally catastrophic. Samuel Blackall, the newly appointed governor of Queensland, was a well-travelled man with a military background who had turned to administrative positions, serving as governor in Sierra Leone between 1862 and 1865, then named "Governor-in-chief of the African Settlements", a broad and as it turned out temporary position which had lasted only a couple of years. Queensland was more promising, and the climate was better for his health, which had begun to fail after his service in Africa. He had arrived in Queensland not long after Von Attems' departure, but it was not long before he heard complaints about a certain Prussian nobleman who had left behind him a number of debts and worthless cheques.

The name Von Attems soon struck a chord with him. He had

Von Attems' ship Hamlet's Ghost *at Surabaya, Java, in 1865.*

met a member of that family in Sierra Leone, and indeed as far as could be made out the Prussian had died in the colony and Blackall had attended his funeral. He mentioned this to the local businessmen who now found that their belated suspicions were confirmed. Enquiries in northern Queensland showed that the so-called Count Von Attems had behaved in Bowen and Somerset as he had in Brisbane, but that the *Hamlet's Ghost* had left Australia and was on its way to the Dutch East Indies. Governor Blackall dealt with the matter promptly by sending a message to the Dutch authorities in Batavia, as present-day Jakarta was then known. There was no schooner identifiable as the *Hamlet's Ghost* at anchor in Batavia, so messages were sent to other ports, including Surabaya. It was only a matter of days before the impressive Count Von Attems, who had been strutting around the town and already incurring debts, was placed under arrest.

It took some time before the questioning produced any information of value. The impostor was a man of great skill and acting talents. He haughtily protested his innocence, blamed the Queensland settlers for spreading lies about him, and rejected the accusations as shameful insults against the greatness of the German empire, of which Prussia was the dominant force. But in time, he cracked under pressure and was forced to admit that he was in no way a member of the Von Attems family, but a mere servant. He was Kurt Oswald Schmaltz, one of the real Count Von Attem's valets, who had left the real Count's employment some years back, and was able to impersonate his master, having learnt a great deal about his contacts and his stylish behaviour. He had left Prussia for the Netherlands, where he had begun his impersonation, and paid his way by issuing bills of exchange in the Count's name.

He was now transferred to Batavia and formally charged with

fraud and grand theft. Further information was obtained about his misdeeds, including some time he had spent in the United States under the name of Count Von Auersperg, and in Egypt where he used the name of Count de Salis, both highly-regarded Austrian families. He was eventually sentenced to over 20 years' imprisonment. The *Hamlet's Ghost* was sold, fetching a modest sum, and the crew members were left to work their way back to Australia. According to one story, Von Attems sent his famous boots to one of his debtors in Brisbane, whether as part settlement of the considerable sum he owed him, which would never be repaid, or as a joke.

Schmaltz escaped at least twice and was recaptured. There is a report of a third escape that led to his disappearance, but so little can be confirmed about this famous impostor that this may be as fictitious as the rest of his claims.

16

Father Rougier
Missionary and Businessman

The Pacific Ocean, with its multitude of islands, was an early destination for missionaries. The Spanish were naturally among the first, with the notable example of Pedro Fernandez de Quiros, who spent most of his life struggling to discover and evangelise the non-existent southern continent and its outlying islands. The arrival of Dutch, British and French explorers and settlers led to the presence of missionaries of various denominations. Most of these were successful, although a number lost their lives as the result of attacks by islanders and various illnesses, while rivalries between the two main denominations, Protestant and Catholic, caused problems in various districts.

One of the leading groups was the Marist order, set up in France in 1816 and soon entrusted by the Pope with the task of developing missions in the Pacific world. They were most successful, although they suffered heavy losses in their early years, including the murder – or martyrdom – of Fr Pierre Chanel on the island of Futuna in 1841. The growth of Christianity throughout the islands led to a frequent restructuring of the administrative framework, including in

1887 the foundation of a Vicariate of the Fiji Islands. This required the recruitment of new missionaries, and the newly-appointed Vicar, Monsignor Julien Vidal, travelled to France to meet potential volunteers. One of these was 23-year-old Emmanuel Rougier, who had just completed his second year of theological studies.

Father Rougier

Rougier was the son of a pious couple from the village of La Chomette in the Auvergne. They had encouraged him to work hard and enter the church, but he had a sense of adventure and a desire to see the world; he was therefore only too happy to join Vidal and sail with him to Fiji. He arrived in Suva in August 1888 and at once displayed the energy and ambition for which he later became famous. He learnt the local language and travelled around the islands, gathering groups of faithful who in many cases had been converted by the Methodist missionaries, organised schools and built small chapels. Vidal naturally appreciated his work, but became concerned when the British administrator complained to him that Rougier had celebrated his successes by holding festivals at which bonfires were lit using Methodist bibles!

Rougier took little notice of his superior's warning, and in 1892 he travelled to Sydney and to New Caledonia, where he asked the local bishop, Monsignor Fraisse, for permission to buy land on Pentecost Island in the New Hebrides, where he built a church and a rectory. He settled for a while in this diocese, where he seems to have done some trading as well as his required parish work, but eventually handed this over to another missionary and returned to Fiji. Rumours about business activities seem to have continued to circulate for some time, but his work for the church does not appear to have suffered. In 1904, however, an event occurred which changed his life for ever.

This was a meeting with a French former convict, Gustave Cecille, who had been sentenced to five years' imprisonment for desertion while serving with the army in Algeria. After serving his time, he had gradually made his way to the township of Levuka, on Ovalau Island. It had been an important early settlement, with a population of about 800 residents, mainly traders, shipwrights, a mission station, and vagabonds like himself. Originally regarded as the administrative capital of the Fiji islands, a status it held until the late 1870s when Suva took over, it had become a peaceful and prosperous corner of the South Pacific. When Rougier visited the place and met Cecille, the two became close friends, and the former convict was quite happy to join Rougier in Viti Levu and, among other things, help him build a church.

Vidal was not so happy to learn of the growing friendship between a man of such dubious character and his increasingly troublesome local priest. He was even more displeased when he heard that Fr Rougier had celebrated the wedding of Cecille with a young Fijian woman. But Rougier took no notice of his superior, and when Cecille asked whether it was possible to obtain some information about his family back in France, he was only too willing to help. To their surprise, they discovered that his parents had died, but had left a considerable sum to their unfortunate son. Cecille had no wish to return to France, something which anyhow was not too easy for a former deserter and convict, and he asked Rougier to help him to negotiate with the French legal authorities. Rougier decided to go to France to deal with this matter. A family member would assist to establish Cecille's claim to the fortune, and to Vidal's shock, Rougier took the Fijian wife with him, without bothering to ask his superior's permission.

Rougier was successful in ensuring that Cecille's inheritance was passed on to him, but the convict was not skilled enough to handle the finances, and he promptly came to an agreement with the missionary, by which Rougier would grant him an annual allowance and deal with the capital and the balance of the yearly income as he wished. Vidal expressed his displeasure at this turn of events, but Rougier as usual took little notice.

A complex situation had developed in two atolls of modern-day Kiribati, which were known at the time as Fanning and Washington Islands, both discovered in 1798 by the American trader and explorer Edmund Fanning. They were uninhabited at the time, but were gradually settled and became relatively important sites for coconut plantations. Fanning, or Tahanea, was annexed by the United Kingdom in 1888, and Washington, or Teraina, which had been claimed by the United States in 1856, became nominally a British possession in 1889. However, by the early 1900s the price of copra had fallen, and the landowners were suffering. The islands were put up for sale by auction: Rougier bought them up and founded a company he named The Fanning Island Company.

He also bought a schooner to enable him to trade between the islands and Honolulu or Australia. This was totally unacceptable to Vidal, who told Rougier to choose between his missionary role and his business activities. Rougier appealed to the Marist authorities in France, but for once he was turned down and told to leave the order, although he could still retain his rights as a priest. Cutting all links with Vidal and his diocese, he moved to Tahiti where he could more easily supervise the reconstruction of trade on Fanning and Washington.

This was done most effectively, and Rougier was able to sell the two islands in 1911, making a substantial profit. That same year, Gustave Cecille died, and Rougier signed an agreement with his widow whereby she received a yearly pension while he continued to run the business. She remarried shortly after, to a Fijian, and dropped out of the picture. Rougier, left in sole charge, free from the nagging comments of his bishop and disposing of large cash assets, decided to buy another island, Christmas Island.

Part of the Kiribati group and known by its local name of Kiritimati, Christmas was a substantial island, almost 400 square kilometres in area, which had been discovered in 1537 by the Spanish explorer Hernando de Grijalva. Although it was claimed for a while by the United States as part of the so-called Guano Islands, it remained largely uninhabited and undeveloped until the 1880s. Settlers gradually established plantations of coconuts, and fishermen used it as a base for whaling and other activities, and its future looked promising. However, droughts and poor management led to eventual failures. It required a man of total dedication and inflexible character like Rougier to rescue it. He set up a company in London under the impressive name of The Central Pacific Coconut Plantation Company, thus ensuring that traders and dealers would feel respect towards his endeavours, and he moved in with a group of 25 Chinese and 20 Tahitians to develop the potential that Christmas Island possessed. He planted upwards of 800,000 coconut trees, built a home for himself which he called "Paris", but spent a good deal of his time doing business in Papeete, where he was becoming increasingly respected, and assisted the local Catholic missionaries. To run the Christmas Island plantations on a daily basis, he appointed a friend named Joe English as his resident manager.

Although the island prospered with the price of copra rising, the First World War soon isolated it from the rest of the Pacific. Travel to Tahiti became well-nigh impossible, there were rumours of German raiders in various parts of the Pacific and Joe English, even with the help of his two sons, found his position difficult and worrying. When Lord Jellicoe visited the island in 1919 on his way to New Zealand, English, still unsure that the war had actually ended in November 1918, drew his pistol and threatened the officers who were attempting to land. He was glad to leave the island, having ensured that the vast stores of copra were safely despatched to Tahiti. Father Rougier thanked him and appointed in his stead Michel Coulon, a demobbed member of the French air force.

Coulon was an able administrator – once he managed to reach his post! He had sailed from Papeete in the small schooner *Tamarii Moorea* whose captain was ill – some said driven insane by the heat and some tropical disease – and who found it impossible to chart his way to Christmas Island. The schooner drifted on to the atoll of Nukunonu in the Tokelaus, where the small crew were able to get help, but were forced to make their way back to Papeete. However, once he did reach Christmas Island, he proved himself a skilled and hard-working manager and ran the plantations until 1927. The enterprise was so successful that one finds it on occasion referred to as "Treasure Island".

Father Rougier had meanwhile bought a schooner of his own, the *Luka*, which he used for trading between the various islands and ferrying copra back from Christmas Island to Papeete. Prohibition had been introduced in the United States, following the passing of the 18th amendment to the constitution which banned "the manufacture, sale, or transportation of intoxicating liquors". This offered a great opportunity for contraband, including from the Pacific side. Rougier was among the first to organise this and he rented a three-master for the purpose. It was impressively named the *Marechal Foch* after the great French war hero, and it could sail confidently along the Californian coast, openly selling copra and other Pacific goods, and less openly numberless gallons of alcohol.

With Cecille long dead and no one to challenge him, Father Rougier had acquired a great deal of wealth and an apparently unchallengeable status throughout the French and British Pacific territories. Although the Marists still muttered at times against him, he silenced most Christian critics by cash donations. But as far as the authorities were concerned, Emmanuel Rougier was highly regarded. Those who criticised his methods were, like their religious counterparts, silenced with gifts or soft-spoken threats.

Christmas Island postage stamps issued by Father Rougier.

Admiral Decoux, a former French High Commissioner, describes him living in his estate at Tanoe, "a *paterfamilias* surrounded by natives of both sexes who respected him as their benefactor and mentor". He was chairman of the agricultural association and chairman of the newly-founded Society of Oceanian Studies.

His ownership of Christmas Island was unquestioned, and he was often referred to as "The King of Christmas Island". This, to some extent, went to his head when he began to issue banknotes and postage stamps. The banknotes presented few problems, as they were regarded locally as the equivalent of cheques issued by him or his trading company, and like any form of currency they needed to be exchanged by a bank if anyone wanted to use the currency of another country: they might have some validity in Tahiti where the locals knew Rougier, but they would not be of any use in Australia or the United States. Postage stamps, however, were a different matter. They were of no significance on Christmas Island, where there was no real postal service, or in French Polynesia,

One of Father Rougier's banknotes.

but their use for postal services abroad and their significance for stamp collectors was another question. International postal services had come under the jurisdiction of the Universal Postal Union created in 1874 and based in Switzerland. It is now part of the United Nations services and ensures that international postal services are properly run. Recognising official postal systems implied recognition as an independent country, a function which it continues to this very day as the world political situation changes and new territories gain their independence. The officials in charge in the first half of the 20th century had no problem dealing with Father Rougier's Christmas Island: they confirmed that it was part of the British possessions in the Pacific, and it had no power to issue its own stamps. Rougier was reported to be furious at this decision, not because there was any mail of any significance being sent out of Christmas Island, but because he saw in it a continuing source of income from the growing number of world philatelists.

Samples of the stamps he had designed still exist, with a modest market as curios, and show his attempt to get around the question of national independence: they are labelled "Cocoanut Plantations Ltd, Central Pacific, Mailboat Service", but they can only be regarded as labels.

As the years passed, Rougier endeavoured to pass on his business to younger family members. A nephew, Paul Rougier, came out from France to take over Christmas Island, but he lacked his uncle's smooth and skilful manners, tended to bully the workers, and was even rumoured to have shot two Tahitians. Father Rougier died on 16 December 1932, aged 68, and his nephew was left in charge in his place, but he soon found himself in trouble. The Great Depression of the mid-1930s did not help matters. Father Rougier had invested large sums in an Asian bank, the China Foo, which went bankrupt, and in the equally unfortunate trading enterprise, Kong Ha. There were rumours of thefts and shady dealings, which some tended to blame on Paul Rougier. He totally lacked the personality and contacts his uncle had built up over the years. The former missionary's reputation began once again to be questioned by locals and by those he had dealt with in Australia and the United States. As rumours of an impending war began to circulate, Paul Rougier felt it was safer for him to return to France, and Christmas Island fell back into its isolation, until it became briefly an American wartime base and, later, one for the nuclear experiment that marked the eastern Pacific for a number of years.

Father Emmanuel Rougier was buried in Tahiti, and an imposing tomb had been built for him, dominated by a large granite cross. He had come to the Pacific as a missionary, and in spite of all his shady dealings and questionable financial manoeuvres, had never been averse to using this status to help his commercial operations.

Settlement and coconut plantation on Fanning Island.

When, in 1949, one of his nieces arrived in Suva to claim his estate, including his supposed ownership of Christmas Island, she was well received, and the British High Commission agreed to pay the Rougiers the sum of 50,000 pounds sterling for the atoll of which he had once claimed to be the king. She left the question of the Christmas Island postage stamps aside – she knew that Father Emmanuel had come out to the Pacific with nothing, having taken the usual vow of poverty, and she was only too glad to go back to France with this substantial legacy.

17

Niels Sorensen

As we have noted, by the middle of the 19th century, the Pacific Ocean was becoming sufficiently well known for traders and investors to consider it as a region vast enough to offer opportunities for making considerable profit and setting up outposts of commercial importance. At the same time, European nations were looking at it as an area of islands and island groups large enough to be colonised. This often created a situation in which unscrupulous merchants came face to face with administrators appointed to develop colonial outposts and establish firm links with the local inhabitants. There was, accordingly, a period during which what some might claim as international laws came into existence, increasingly backed by units of naval forces. However, the growth in trade and the exploitation of the Pacific world's resources also provided opportunities for crafty and unscrupulous operators to sneak in and carry out fraudulent deals.

Among the various characters who wormed their way around the growing Pacific world from the 1870s to the early 20th century was Niels Peder Sorensen, a man of Danish origin, whose background is difficult to establish with any precision because he apparently forged most of his papers, including his birth certificate. In his later years, when he was endeavouring to qualify for an American invalid pension, he stated that he was born in a Danish town on 4 January 1848, but had made his way to New York at the age of 11, possibly as a ship's boy, had managed to survive on his own and subsequently served on two United States vessels during the Civil War. His application was turned down because of incorrect or confusing details, but it does seem that he had enlisted in the American Navy some time in 1867, by which time he was 19. He served in three different vessels and made a voyage to Asia in one of them before being discharged in 1870. He then turned to the merchant navy, serving on various vessels and occasionally changing his name to Peter Pederson, an anglicised version of his own first name, which he adopted from another sailor who had served with him on the USS *Piscataqua*.

In 1873, he was serving as boatswain on a merchantman which

Christchurch in 1875.

had crossed the Atlantic to England and on its way back was taking emigrants to New Zealand. One of these was a 21-year-old Englishwoman called Annie Smith, with whom he fell in love. He discharged himself from the crew when the vessel put into Christchurch, got a job as a sawmiller, and married her. They had two children and moved to Auckland where Sorensen worked as a diver. They separated some years later, Sorensen simply walking away from the family and sailing off on his own.

In March 1877, he was offered work as a diver on the schooner *Mary Anderson* which was setting off for New Caledonia and other Pacific islands to collect pearl shells and copra. The *Mary Anderson* was in fact one of many trading vessels going from island to island looking for business, taking islanders to work as labourers in the New Hebrides, buying copra and food supplies, carrying timber and fishing. The captain was an enterprising man, Harry Shipman, as was his supercargo, Hamilton Wright, and they often clashed with Sorensen whom they accused of dealing for his own benefit, of ignoring instructions, and of brutality towards the islanders with whom they had to deal. They decided to leave Sorensen at Cockatoo Island, a diving and trading post in Thousand Ships Bay at the south-western end of the Solomon island of Santa Isabel. Sorensen was officially in charge of the station, collecting shells and other items which the *Mary Anderson* was expected to pick up on a return visit.

The first vessel to put into Cockatoo Island after Sorensen's arrival was an Anglican mission ship, the *Southern Cross*. Sorensen came on board and attended a service, but a minister, the Reverend Alfred Penny, expressed his surprise at Sorensen carrying a loaded revolver in his belt. It was later discovered that he had brutalised a number of islanders during his stay on the island, flogging at least one man who worked at the station and shooting another, so that he needed to defend himself from a possible revenge attack. Shipman and Wright, returning in the *Mary Anderson*, decided to close the station which showed no prospects, especially in the atmosphere that had developed since Sorensen's arrival. Things did not improve as the vessel continued its voyage and Sorensen, who naturally had rejoined them after leaving Cockatoo Island, was put ashore, "drunk and riotous" as the captain and supercargo reported. They intended to leave him behind; however, they too were found to be the worse for alcohol and in a quarrelsome mood. The British authorities were endeavouring to increase their influence in the region and ensure the islands they were working to colonise would no longer have to suffer from ill-treatment by roaming traders. Consequently, an officer from HMS *Beagle* came along to carry out the investigation, drew up a report on the happenings on board, and ordered the *Mary Anderson* to take Sorensen back on board, sail to New Zealand with the cargo they had managed to collect, and report to the authorities there.

An investigation was carried out in Auckland by the Collector of Customs, but the evidence against Sorensen was insufficient for his behaviour to lead to any firm prosecution. Sorensen simply told the investigations that he had merely acted in accordance with his captain's instructions, and that if anything he had done could be considered as unfair or excessive, then Wright was to blame. There were no witnesses to call for evidence, and the matter was dropped. Sorensen was allowed to work in Auckland for some five or six years, then made his way to Australia, and in April 1884 sailed for the Pacific islands, mostly the Solomons, working as a diver on the two-masted schooner *Albert*, collecting pearl shell and copra. The ship was back in Sydney by late January 1885 after a successful voyage, but once again accusations were made about Sorensen's behaviour. The naval vessel HMS *Diamond* had stopped the *Albert* to enquire about rumours of illegal passengers and possible murders. After some hesitation, the captain had admitted that they had taken a total of four Solomon Islanders to work the diving pump, who had fled after a while, escaping to another island where they had been attacked and killed by the locals. The officer from the *Diamond* reminded the captain that he had no authority to employ islanders and that the days when labourers could be taken from their homes were now over, but he took no further action.

However, when the *Albert* completed its journey in Sydney, crewmen reported that the Solomon Islanders had fled because of constant ill-treatment by Sorensen who beat them, overworked them, and denied them food when he felt dissatisfied with their work. They also said there had been more than three islanders involved, five having been taken from the islet of Gaeta and another from Guadalcanal who had been kept in irons by Sorensen, his few belongings being sold to other islanders for his master's profit. The problem was that these victims were not available to testify at a trial, and that the only witnesses who might be able to come forward were sailors from the *Albert*, which was about to sail off on another voyage. To make matters even more complicated, the ownership of the *Albert* was nominally transferred to a local Portuguese resident. This was done with the collusion of the Portuguese consul who received a small fee to record the ship as a Portuguese vessel, henceforth to be known as the *Douro*. This struck the Australian authorities as somewhat suspicious, but it made it impossible for them to prevent the ship and her crew from leaving Sydney and for Sorensen to be prosecuted for any illegal action. The excuse put forward by the *Albert*'s captain was that the transfer would save the ship from being seized if a conflict broke out between Russia and Great Britain, something which was rumoured at the time. Sorensen, now master of the *Douro*, sailed away in April with a cargo of trade goods to sell to islanders and settlers. An article in the *Brisbane Courier* reported Sorensen as saying: "I'm now out of English law; I am my own master; I can trade now with what I like – with rifle, cartridge, powder and dynamite".

Reaching Marau on Guadalcanal, Sorensen recruited – or tricked on board – several islanders, and then a further seven at Cockatoo Island, off Santa Isabel. A little while later, he captured another islander at Wagina, near the island of Choiseul, and found that this was a local chief. He decided that it would be more profitable to treat him as a prisoner than as a potential worker, and he bargained with the islanders for his freedom, receiving 4,000 bêche-de-mer, 24 turtle shells, one pig, and three islanders to work on the *Douro*. He realised that it was more profitable to kidnap prisoners, take canoes or other possessions from the islanders, and give them back in exchange for local goods. He even claimed that he could purchase some small island to establish an outpost of his own. These straightforward acts of piracy, accompanied by brutality towards his own men – the ship's cook was beaten by Sorensen and lost five teeth in the attack – led his crewmen to worry about their own fate, and towards the end of June, several of them absconded from the *Douro* and set off in a longboat for a coaling station where they hoped to find British naval authorities to whom they could report Sorensen's actions.

They did not find the officials they were hoping for, but they were helped by the captain of a trading vessel who took them eventually to Sydney. They told their story, which the *Sydney Morning Herald* published in a lengthy article entitled "Outrages in the South Seas". The case was taken up by Admiral George Tryon, who had already been investigating the transfer of the *Douro* in what was believed by many locals to have been an illegal transaction. He asked the colonial authorities to arrest Sorensen if they came across him, aware that the *Douro* was continuing to sail around the islands. Sorensen by then was looting islanders in the Admiralty group, north of New Guinea, where in mid-October he had invited several canoes to come out and trade, and as soon as they approached the *Douro* had fired at them, causing the natives to jump overboard and swim back to land, whereupon he had seized all the goods they had brought out and destroyed the canoes. He continued in this manner for another couple of months before returning to Australia, where he was at last placed under arrest in December 1885.

Sorensen came to trial four months later, but argued that he did not come under Australian jurisdiction because he was a Danish citizen and his ship was a Portuguese vessel. Both claims were rejected and this time enough crewmen could be found to give evidence and detail his misdeeds. He was sentenced to 10 years' imprisonment for robbery and assault, and the *Douro*, once again known as the *Albert*, was forfeited to the Crown. One of the reasons for Sorensen's conviction was the Portuguese consul's decision to protect his own interests by turning against him and testifying that the transfer of the *Albert* to Sorensen was illegal and further proof of the man's deviousness. Sorensen served most of his sentence in Queensland's St Helena prison, and was released in March 1894.

Managing to find a few jobs to sustain himself for a couple of years around Australia and across to North America, Sorensen is recorded as endeavouring to persuade speculators in New South Wales and in Canada to invest in a scheme to search for gold in the Solomon Islands. He succeeded in creating an exploration company based in San Francisco, which he called the South Sea Commercial Company, to search for copper, gold and sea pearls in the Solomons. Gold mining was particularly alluring as this was the time of the famous Klondike goldrush, and he succeeded in persuading several American businessmen to invest the substantial sum of $16,000. This enabled him to buy a three-masted schooner, the *Sophia Sutherland*, in which he sailed in September 1897 with a group of hopeful followers. According to newspaper reports, they intended to spend up to three years in the Solomons, gathering pearl shells and prospecting for gold. On board were adequate supplies for the voyage, including muskets which would keep under control any Solomon Islanders who might object to their presence. The captain was Alexander McLean, renowned in the Pacific world as a skilled mariner and seal hunter, but also as a ruthless thief and smuggler.

They reached Apia in Samoa in October, where the American consul warned McLean to beware of Sorensen whose reputation in the islands as a brutal and dishonest trader was well-known. They then went on to Tulagi in the Solomon group and finally landed at Rennell Island, which Sorensen had advertised as a sure source of gold and copper. They prospected there for two months, found little evidence of valuable minerals since the island was mostly coral, but took rock samples back to Tulagi to be analysed. The assayer found only the minutest traces of gold, which he assessed as equal to no more than about four shillings' worth per ton. The once-optimistic gold-miners then turned against Sorensen and started beating him up, until he tried to produce a document appointing himself as the owner and trader in charge of the *Sophia Sutherland*. They thrust his claims aside, pointing that it was their money which had made the expedition and the purchase of the schooner possible, and set him ashore to be taken to Australia by a passing ship. They then went on their way, carried out a little trading and, giving up when most of the crew and would-be miners were struck down by malaria and scurvy, returned to San Francisco.

Sorensen had managed to find employment as a boatswain aboard the coal carrier *Bedford* which was on its way from New South Wales to America, and reached San Francisco in June 1898. He gave people a carefully edited version of the *Sophia Sutherland*'s voyage, but when Alexander McLean returned to San Francisco, Sorensen promptly vanished, and was not heard of for several years. He reappeared several years later, when he endeavoured unsuccessfully to obtain a pension as a former and now invalid soldier of the American Civil War. But in 1908, he rose to prominence in New York with a proposal to organise a company to recover the large quantity of gold lost when the *General Grant*, on her way from Australia to Britain, had sunk somewhere to the south of New Zealand. He claimed to have a map which showed where the wreck lay, and that the cargo was worth at least 20 million dollars. He was recognised by a journalist from the *New York Sun*, William Churchill, who remembered his misdeeds in the Pacific and wrote a detailed article recounting the story of the *Douro* and of the *Sophia Sutherland*. Churchill warned that financing another expedition with Sorensen in charge would be disastrous. Sorensen, deciding that it was easier to get money from the newspaper than from potential investors, sued the *Sun* for libel and sought 100,000 dollars in damages.

The case came to trial in March 1911, but the jury was split so that a second trial had to be scheduled; however, Sorensen agreed to drop the matter, receiving no doubt some compensation from the *Sun* for his legal costs. He then moved to New Zealand and tried to raise funds for another search for the treasure of the *General Grant*. When that was unsuccessful, he tried to sell an island in the Solomons which he claimed to have bought in 1885 from a local chief. He actually travelled to the Solomons in June 1913, but the Resident Commissioner threatened to have him arrested and deported if he tried to land. He then sailed on to the Shortland Islands to the south of Bougainville, where the local authorities also forbade him to land and finally issued a formal deportation order banning him from further attempts to lay claim to land or to trade.

Sorensen reappeared in 1925 when he wrote to the British Prime Minister, Stanley Baldwin, protesting against the banning order and outlining a new proposal for a plan to develop part of the Solomons. The authorities took no notice of him, but in 1929 he put forward a claim on behalf of a company he apparently held, called the United States Treasury Islands Incorporated. Enquiries showed that this was little more than a paper company, supposedly owned by a resident of New York. This was Sorensen's last attempt to raise money from gullible investors, something he had been doing for years to maintain himself. But he was now in his eighties, and regarded by some as a senile old man, although he still possessed the gift for evoking the golden image of a Pacific Ocean full of promise for anyone willing to invest in a grandiose scheme. He died in New York in February 1935.

Select Bibliography

Alexander, Caroline, *The Bounty: The True Story of the Mutiny on the* Bounty, Penguin, New York, 2003.

Allen, H.R., *Buccaneer Admiral Sir Henry Morgan*, Arthur Baker, London, 1976.

Baudoin, A., *L'Aventure de Port-Breton et la colonie libre de la Nouvelle-France*, Dreyfus, Paris, 1883.

Baumard, Louis and Guillou, Jean, *Aventures dans les mers du sud: Marins, explorateurs et trafiquants au coeur du Pacifique*, L'Etrave, Beauvoir-sur-mer, 2003.

Bethune, C.R.D. (ed.), *The Observations of Sir Richard Hawkins, Knt, in his Voyage into the South Sea in the Year 1593*, Hakluyt Society, London, 1847.

Boulagnon, Pierre, *Emmanuel Rougier, des isles d'Auvergne à l'Océanie*, Ed. de Roure, Polignac, 2002.

Bromby, R., *German Raiders of the South Seas*, Doubleday, Hong Kong, 1985.

Clements, Jonathan, *Coxinga and the Fall of the Ming Dynasty*, Sutton, Stroud, 2005.

Coote, Stephen, *Drake: The Life and Legend of an Elizabethan Hero*, Simon & Schuster, Sydney, 2003.

Daudet, Alphonse, *Port Tarascon: Dernières aventures de L'Illustre Tartarin*, Paris, 1890.

Defoe, Daniel, *The Life and Strange Surprizing Adventures of Robinson Crusoe, of York, Mariner*, London, 1719.

Dening, Greg, *Mr Bligh's Bad Language: Passion, Power and Theatre on the* Bounty, Cambridge, 1992.

Detmers, Theodore, *The Raider* Kormoran, William Kimber, London, 1959.

Dunmore, John, *Chasing a Dream: The Exploration of the Imaginary Pacific*, Upstart Press, Auckland, 2016.

Dunmore, John, *Who's Who in Pacific Navigation*, Melbourne University Press, Melbourne, 1992.

Dunmore, John, *Wild Cards: Eccentric Characters from New Zealand's Past*, New Holland, Auckland, 2006.

Durand, Jules, *Bois d'Ebène*, Paris, 1900.

Estensen, Miriam, *Terra Australis Incognita: The Spanish Quest for the Mysterious Great South Land*, Allen & Unwin, Crows Nest, Australia, 2006.

Exquemelin, Alexandre Olivier, *Bucaniers of America...wherein are contained more especially the Unparalleled Exploits of Sir Henry Morgan*, 2 vols, Wm Crooke, London, 1684.

Festetics de Tolna, Rudolf, *Chez les Cannibales: Huit ans de croisière dans le Pacifique*, Plon, Paris, 1903.

George, Neville, *The* Peruvian *and James Morrill: The Story of the* Peruvian *shipwrecked in 1846 and the Survivor James Morrill*, Townsville Museum, Queensland, 1989.

Gibson, Gregory, *Demon of the Waters: The True Story of the Mutiny on the Whaleship* Globe, Hodder Headline, Sydney, 2002.

Gibson, Walter M., *The Prison of Weltevreden: and a Glance at the East Indian Archipelago*, Sampson Low, London, 1856.

Guillou, Jean, *Echos du Grand Océan*, L'Etrave, Le Fresne, 2006.

Guillou, Jean, *Les Mers du Sud m'ont raconté*, Le Fresne, 2008.

Heffernan, Thomas Farel, *Mutiny on the* Globe: *The Fatal Voyage of Samuel Comstock*, Norton & Co, New York, 2002.

Horne, Gerald, *The White Pacific: U.S. Imperialism and Black Slavery in the South Seas after the Civil War*, University of Hawaii Press, 2007.

Hoyt, E.P., *Count Von Lucknow: Knight of the Sea*, McKay, New York, 1969.

Hoyt, E.P., *Mutiny on the* Globe, Barker, London, 1976.

Hussey, Cyrus M., and Lay, William, *A Narrative of the Mutiny, on board the Ship* Globe, *of Nantucket, in the Pacific Ocean, January 1824*, New London, Connecticut, 1828.

Kelsey, Harry, *Sir Francis Drake: The Queen's Pirate*, Yale, New Haven, 1998.

Kennedy, Gavin, *Captain Bligh: The Man and his Mutinies*, Duckworth & Co., London, 1989.

Kraska, Robert, *The Strange but True Adventures of Alexander Selkirk, the True Robinson Crusoe*, Clarion Books, New York, 2005.

Lansdown, Richard (ed.), *Strangers in the South Seas: The Idea of the Pacific in Western Thought*, University of Hawaii, Honolulu, 2006.

Laracy, Hugh, *Watriama and Co: Further Pacific Islands Portraits*, ANU Press, Canberra, 2013.

Maude, H.E., "In Search of a Home: From the Mutiny to Pitcairn Island", in *Journal of the Polynesian Society 67/2*, pp. 104–31.

McKee, Alexander, *The Queen's Corsair: Drake's Journey of Circumnavigation 1577–1580*, Souvenir Press, London, 1978.

McNally, Michael, *Coronel and Falklands 1914*, Osprey Publishing, Oxford, 2012.

Merland, Constant, *Dix-sept Ans chez les sauvages: Aventures de Narcisse Pelletier*, Dentu, Paris, 1876.

Mitchener, James, A. & Grove Day, *Rascals in Paradise*, Random House, New York, 1957.

Niau, J.H., *The Phantom Paradise: The Story of the Expedition of the Marquis de Rays*, Angus and Robertson, Sydney, 1937.

Parkinson, Richard, ed. by Peter White, *Thirty Years in the South Seas; Land, People, Customs and Traditions in the Bismarck Archipelago and on the German Solomon Islands*, Hurst & Co, London, 1999.

Paulding, Hiram, *Journal of a Cruise of the United States Schooner Dolphin in Pursuit of the Mutineers of the Whale Ship* Globe, G. & C. Carvill, New York, 1831.

Preston, Diana and Michael, *A Pirate of Exquisite Mind; The Life of William Dampier, Explorer, Naturalist and Buccaneer*, Doubleday, London, 2004.

Raphalen, Daniel, *L'Odysée de Port-Breton, ou le rêve océanien du Marquis de Rays*, Portes du Large, 1986.

Ringrose, Basil, *The Dangerous Voyage and Bold Assaults of Captain Bartholomew Sharp and Others*, London, 1684.

Ringrose, Basil, ed. by Derek Howse and Norman Thrower, *A Buccaneer's Atlas: Basil Ringrose's South Sea Waggoner*, University of California Press, Berkeley, 1992.

Robinson, Stephen, *False Flags: Disguised Raiders of World War II*, Exisle, Auckland, 2016.

Robson, Robert Williams, *Queen Emma; The Samoan-American Girl who Founded an Empire on 19th Century New Guinea*, Pacific Publications, Sydney, 1965.

Rogers, Woodes, *A Cruizing Voyage Round the World*, Andrew Bell, London, 1712.

Rosenman, Helen, *An Account in Two Volumes of Two Voyages to the South Seas by Jules S.C. Dumont d'Urville*, Melbourne University Press, 1987.

Rutter, Owen, *The Court-martial of the "Bounty" Mutineers*, Hodge & Co., Edinburgh, 1931.

Salmond, Anne, *Bligh: William Bligh in the South Seas*, Penguin Viking, Auckland, 2011.

Scarr, Deryck, *A History of the Pacific Islands: Passages through Tropical Times*, Routledge, London, 2002.

Schreiberg, Roy E., *The Fortunate Adversities of William Bligh*, Peter Lang, New York, 1991.

Schurtz, William L., *The Manila Galleon*, E.P. Dutton, New York, 1959.

Sternbeck, Alfred, *Filibusters and Buccaneers,* Methuen, London, 1930.

Thomas, Lowell Jackson, *The Sea Devil: The Story of Felix von Luckner, the German War Raider*, Heinemann, London, 1927.

Thomson, W.C., *The "Hamlet's Ghost"*, Historical Society of Queensland, Espace Library, University of Queensland, Brisbane, 1916.

Vermont, M.H., *Le Procès du Marquis de Rays*, Marseille, 1884.

Williams, Glyndwr, *The Great South Sea: English Voyages and Encounters 1570–1750*, Yale, New Haven, 1997.

Woodward, D., *The Secret Raiders: The Story of the Operations of the German Armed Merchant Raiders in the Second World War,* William Kimber, London, 1955.

Index